CAMRA'S
Edinburgh
Pub Walks

CAMRA'S
Edinburgh

Pub Walks

BOB STEEL

Published by the Campaign for Real Ale Ltd.
230 Hatfield Road
St Albans
Hertfordshire AL1 4LW
www.camra.org.uk/books

ISBN 978-1-85249-274-8

A CIP catalogue record for this book is
available from the British Library
Printed and bound in China by Latitude Press Ltd

Managing Editor: **Simon Hall**
Project Editor: **Katie Hunt**
Editorial Assistance: **Emma Haines**
Design/Typography: **Stephen Bere**
Cover Design: **Dale Tomlinson**
Cartography: **Stephen Bere**
Marketing Manager: **Kim Carvey**

Photographs: **Bob Steel**
Additional photography: Beltane Fire Society p. 15 (b); Cat Button
pp. 9, 10 (tr), 26 (b), 29, 31 (b), 35 (b); Chris Robson/Scottish Viewpoint pp. 2-3, 79; David Gardiner p. 145; Edinburgh's Hogmanay p.
16 (b); Henriette Gran Myreng pp. 36 (t), 50 (b); Katie Hunt pp. 7, 10
(b), 16 (l), 20, 24, 25 (b), 27 (l, b), 29, 61 (t), 63, 68; Lothian Buses p.
144; Margaret Burgon pp. 123, 124, 125 (b), 126 (b); Mick Slaughter
pp. 8, 12, 13 (l), 20 (l), 21, 22 (t), 26 (b), 30 (b), 46, 134, 137 (b), 139
(t), 141 (t, bru) 142; National Galleries of Scotland p. 49 (t); Pascal
Saez p. 16 (t); Peter Stubbs/www.edinphoto.org.uk p. 36 (b);
The Royal Edinburgh Military Tattoo p. 15 (t)
With thanks to the Abbotsford Bar, Café Royal, Dalriada, Espy,
Four Marys, Guildford Arms, Leslie's Bar, Sheep Heid Inn and
Tyneside Tavern for use of their photography

Cover photography: Top: P.Tomkins/VisitScotland/Scottish Viewpoint; Left: Chris Robson/Scottish Viewpoint; Right: Paul Tomkins/
VisitScotland/Scottish Viewpoint

Acknowledgements
Although this book goes out under my name, it would have been
much the poorer but for the substantial assistance of others. In
particular I'd like to warmly thank members of the Edinburgh & S.E.
Scotland branch of CAMRA who contributed many improvements
to the routes and pub selection; and reviewed the manuscript prior
to publication. Thanks to their assistance I'm confident that errors
have been minimised. I'd especially like to thank Jim Darroch, but
also Fred Chrystal and Roger Preece. Thanks are due to others who
contributed input on particular routes, including James Main, and
Anne Watters of the Kirkcaldy Civic Society.
Bob Steel

Contents

Walk locations

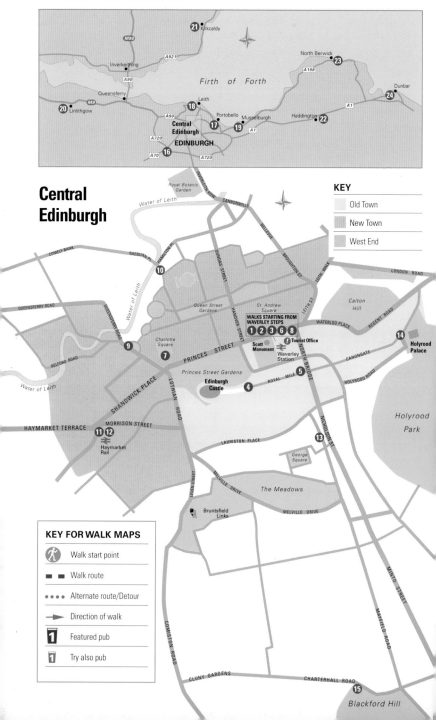

Central Edinburgh

KEY

- Old Town
- New Town
- West End

KEY FOR WALK MAPS

- Walk start point
- Walk route
- Alternate route/Detour
- Direction of walk
- Featured pub
- Try also pub

Introduction

Welcome to CAMRA's Edinburgh Pub Walks. I was very pleased to be asked to work on this book since in my opinion there isn't a more attractive city for urban walks than Edinburgh: it's compact enough to get around very easily on foot and there's a comprehensive bus network to reach areas further afield. Also both the topography and the built landscape offer constantly changing views so that there's always something of interest. Whether it's culture, geology, architecture, history or good food you're interested in, this is a city where you can enjoy your beer in stimulating surroundings and make the most of a day trip or short break in a city with plenty to see and do.

CAMRA is the beer consumers' champion. It was founded in 1971 and continues to grow, with well over 110,000 members. Its main focus remains to promote good quality and well served traditional cask ale, something which almost all of the pubs featured in this guide offer. In addition however CAMRA is also concerned to protect the pubs we drink in, all the more important with the high closure rates of pubs in many parts of the UK. Edinburgh is fortunate to retain numerous traditional pubs with good quality fittings and fine architecture, quite appropriate when the city itself is architecturally one of superlatives. No less an authority than the late great Michael Jackson, aka the 'Beer Hunter' (and not to be confused with the other MJ!) said of Edinburgh that "there is nowhere I would rather pub crawl"

Although Edinburgh at one time was a city of breweries, many of whose names are commemorated in the fine old mirrors you'll see in the city's pubs, the breweries themselves have almost all disappeared. Micro-breweries and brewpubs can spring up quickly but Caledonian at Slateford, part of Scottish and Newcastle, is the only significant

View of Edinburgh Castle from Princes Street Gardens

Sportsman stained glass detail from the Café Royal

retain one of the best sets of worthwhile pub interiors in Britain. Many of these are celebrated in another CAMRA publication: *Scotland's True Heritage Pubs*; and more recently in the Historic Scotland publication 'Raising the bar' available online (only) at www.historic-scotland.gov.uk/raising-the-bar-pubs-booklet.pdf Readers interested in pub interiors are advised to consult both of these to supplement the descriptions contained here. Route 25 (pages 135-42) in this guide is a personal selection of the best of the city's interiors which would make a fine full day tour.

brewer still in the city. You'll find 'Caley' beers, especially the popular straw coloured Deuchars [say 'due cuzz'] IPA very widely available, but the city has always been the best place in Scotland to get a variety of cask ales, and that choice is widening all the time thanks in no small part to the vibrant modern Scottish brewing scene.

The routes

As with any other CAMRA guide, we start with beer quality: of course, not every pint in every pub will be perfect every time; and in some less frequented pubs outside the tourist season the choice of ale may be reduced along with demand; but apart from one or two pubs chosen for their architectural interest, you can expect cask ale to be available in all the pubs in this guide.

Unlike other pub walks books, this guide features several pubs on each route, enabling you to choose the kind of pubs which suit you – or visit them all if you wish! All the routes have public transport information; there's no need to rely on your car for any of them and even the walks in the areas beyond the city are all accessible by train and/or bus. See the sections at the start of each route or transport section on pages 144-5 for more details. Distances are given for all the routes, but it's usually possible either to cut routes short or to link to other adjacent routes if you want a longer walk.

Edinburgh's pub heritage

This leads to another focus of this guide: the growth of interest in pubs with good quality interiors continues, and Edinburgh is fortunate to

Food

As with my *London Pub Walks* book, you'll find general information about food included in the pub information, although of course this can be subject to change at short notice. As a general rule however you should have little difficulty getting decent food on any of the routes in the book.

Disabled access

I regret that as yet access for the disabled is patchy and although the situation is improving, if you are a wheelchair user or you are accompanying somebody who has special access needs, you'll know that the best thing is to ring ahead and ask. For this reason and to avoid potential problems or inaccuracies we haven't included this information in this guide.

Take it easy!

Edinburgh has very liberal opening hours these days, and many pubs and bars will serve beyond midnight, even during the week. Good beer, of course, is best enjoyed at a sensible pace, and for that reason we have avoided the term 'pub crawl'. I prefer to think of a collection of cultural walks washed down with the nation's favourite drink after tea! Please drink responsibly and enjoy the walks.

Bob Steel

The making of a World Heritage city

Walking through Edinburgh, you cannot fail to be impressed by the strong sense of place generated by the variety of urban and natural landscapes. Edinburgh began life, not surprisingly, as a strategic fort on a steep-sided ridge descending eastwards from the Castle Rock, and hemmed in by marshes and lakes – ideal as a defensive site but not so well-suited to a population centre.

It wasn't until the mid 18th century that the city fathers drained the Nor' Loch, by then a putrid lake where Princes Street gardens now lies, and plans were drawn up for a New Town to enable the bourgeoisie to escape the slums. In 1765 work started on a bridge to link the ridge on which the city of Edinburgh was built to the next ridge of land to the north, crossing the Nor' Loch. See the box on page 48 for more detail about the construction of the New Town. In complete contrast to the jumbled tenements clinging to the narrow ridge in the shelter of the castle, the New Town became home to some of the world's most elegant urban architecture. Of special note is the contribution of Robert Adam. His *tour de force*,

Charlotte Square, is the epitome of eighteenth century sophistication, and set a new standard for urban design in Edinburgh. Here he demonstrated his mastery of the difficult task of uniting the facades of a terrace of houses into a single frontage. This theme was carried forward into the so-called Second New Town, laid out to the north of the first in 1802, and subsequent developments such as the Moray Estate, where each block was treated as a single architectural composition in the same fashion as the Charlotte Square terraces. The New Town survives almost intact, and later developments around what is now called the West End continued in the distinctly Scottish urban tradition of

View of Edinburgh from Calton Hill

left: **The superb northern side of Charlotte Square** right: **Scottish Parliament**

handsome villas and well-built stone tenements.

In the 19th century Edinburgh did not become a major manufacturing centre; so it never spawned the large ugly industrial inner-city areas that characterised most British cities, and its architectural heritage was preserved. The only significant manufacturing industries in Edinburgh were printing and brewing: it developed service industries – the banking and legal professions – instead. The downside of this was that it lost its position as Scotland's largest city to Glasgow. The 19th century also saw the construction of most of Edinburgh's landmark monuments and galleries which cemented its place as the cultural as well as the administrative capital of Scotland. Edinburgh would have to wait until 1999 however for the return to Scotland of a

parliament – after a gap of nearly 300 years. The ultra-modern development at the foot of the Royal Mile has been both acclaimed and criticised for its striking design, but its receipt of the RIBA Stirling Prize in 2005 certainly makes it worthy of a chapter in the ongoing story of the construction of Edinburgh.

THE SEVEN HILLS

Like Rome, Edinburgh is said to be built on seven hills: volcanic rocks formed in the Carboniferous and Devonian periods. Glaciation has modified the landscape considerably since the hills were formed but they give Edinburgh its wonderful setting, which is almost unrivalled among major cities.

Each year in late June the Seven Hills Race takes place (see www.seven-hills.org.uk) which, unusually, doesn't follow a marked course but requires participants to summit all seven hills. The seven are Calton Hill (walk 3) and Arthur's Seat (walk 14) – Calton Hill was once structurally part of Arthur's Seat but has since been separated by a geological fault – Castle Rock (walk 4), Craiglockheart Hill, Corstorphine Hill and Blackford and the Braid Hills (walk 15) upon which an information board gives details of the race and the 14 mile course – the current record for which is 1 hour 38 minutes.

Arthur's Seat from Calton Hill

Historic pub interiors

Defending Britain's traditional pubs, as well as its traditional beers, has always been one of CAMRA's declared concerns.

By the early 1980s, when the Campaign set up its Pub Preservation Group, it had become apparent that the nation's pub heritage was being largely ignored by mainstream conservation bodies. Change in pubs has always occurred, and has reflected developments in society; but since the 1960s and 1970s in particular, the British pub has been subject to an accelerated and often destructive wave of internal alterations. A major component of that change has been the opening up of pubs, the removal of screens and partitions, (many of which contained very fine work) and the installation of new, often very inferior, fittings. Safeguarding what is now left of the country's pub heritage has become a very serious conservation challenge. Route 25 will take you to some of the very best pub interiors in Edinburgh, and many of the other pubs on these walks retain historic features that are unique to Scotland.

Characteristics of Scottish pubs

Tenements

One of the most distinctive exterior features of thousands of Scottish pubs and also the most no-ticeable difference between them and pubs in other parts of the UK is that they occupy the ground floors of tenement blocks of flats alongside a variety of shops. Tenements are Scotland's dominant style of urban house building in the European tradition, compared to England, Wales and Ireland where the main style is the terraced house. This means that many Scottish pubs are often little different from adjacent shop-fronts, while pubs in other parts of the UK tend to be the only building on the plot, whether freestanding or part of a terrace. In Scotland, most pubs do not have living accommodation for licensees, due to early 20th-century legislation that made Sunday opening illegal. As a result, pubs were known as 'lock-ups'. Examples include the Barony Bar (walk 3), Clark's Bar (walk 7), Athletic Arms and Roseburn Bar (walk 11), Leslie's Bar (walk 13), and the Station Bar (route 25).

Classic tenement pub, the Roseburn Bar

Island Serving Counters

Up until the 1880s, pubs in Scottish towns and cities had small bar rooms and a number of other sitting rooms, similar to pubs in other parts of the UK. In their classic book *People's Palaces* about the pubs of Scotland in the Victorian and Edward-ian era, Rudolph Kenna and Anthony Mooney state that these old-time pubs were proving unac-ceptable to the licensing magistrates of Glasgow and other Scottish towns and cities, who claimed that the publican and his assistants were unable to exercise overall supervision over their custom-ers. Consequently, many of these pubs were remodeled to create a spacious and often lofty room with a large island serving counter – usually oval in shape but sometimes circular, square or even octagonal – and an ornately carved central fitment holding casks of whisky and occasionally other spirits. The island serving counters at the Abbotsford (walk 6) and Leslie's Bar (walk 13) are unusual in that there is no central fitment to house the spirits, glasses etc. Instead there is a sturdy wooden superstructure on top of the counter. There are a number of other pubs with island serving counters featured in this guide, including the Café Royal (walk 1), Kenilworth (walk 6) and Prestoungrange Gothenburg, Prestonpans (walk 19). Most pubs were designed for this type of stand-up drinking, but some sitting rooms, as they are known, were provided, usually at the front of the pub, and well lit to meet the approval of the authorities.

Ornate Gantries with Spirit Casks

From the 1890s, a number of pubs were refitted with a straight bar counter and an ornately carved fitting behind, holding polished spirit casks and decorated with mirrored centre-pieces, often advertising brewery or distillery products. This fitting is known as a 'gantry', de-rived from 'gantress', or 'gauntress', an old Scots words to describe a wooden stand for casks, which you can find mounted both vertically and on their sides. A number of examples of gantries can also be found in Ireland, which, like Scotland, has a long history of spirit drinking. Ornate gantries complete with spirit casks can be found at Bennet's Bar, Tollcross (walk 8), and the Volunteer Arms (Staggs), Musselburgh (walk 19). Other impressive gantries can be seen in H P

Feuars Arms, Kirkcaldy

Kenilworth, Rose Street

Mather's Bar (walk 2) and Ryrie's Bar (walk 12).

In the past, whisky was brought from the distillery in bulk and blended on the premises, with the finished blend transferred from pub cellars using a water engine (see page 13) to the barrels on the gantry ready to be served. In most pubs in Scotland this practice generally ceased in the interwar period.

Tiled Paintings

There are impressive displays of Victorian tiling to be found in Edinburgh's pubs. The Café Royal (walk 1) has a splendid display of nine Doulton's tiled murals, seven are of famous inventors each at their moment of their discovery. The Barony Bar (walk 3) has a tiled dado including four small pictorial panels of rural Scottish scenes that are, sadly, mostly hidden by seating. Also, in Leith the Central Bar walls are completely covered with tiles by Minton Hollins, including four tiled panels of sporting scenes – yacht racing, hare-coursing, golf and shooting. The walls of the Kenilworth (walk 6) are covered in blue and white Minton tiles, topped-off with rows of brown and white tiles. In Kirkcaldy the Feuars Arms (walk 21) has two-tone tiled walls, including two small Doulton's of Lambeth tiled panels (each a single tile) featuring a jester evidently eyeing up the shepherdess a few feet away; also the long bar counter is completely fronted with brown Art Nouveau tiles.

Pub room names
Sitting Room

Not all Scottish pubs are single spaces. There are many that retain separate rooms termed 'sitting rooms'; where they are very small, we refer to them as 'snugs'. These rooms point up the contrast between respectable seated drinking that would take place therein, as opposed to the 'stand-up drinking' to be expected in the rest of the premises. Occasionally, these rooms can be called 'private', as can be seen in the door glass at Athletic Arms (walk 11) but, sadly, the room division here was removed recently.

left: **Barony Bar, mirror**   right: **The serving hatch at the tiny jug bar at Bennet's Bar, Tollcross**

Family Department

There still exist a number of the tiny rooms, or booths, where drink was bought for consumption off the premises: the purchasers were often women, even children, who were sent to the pub to collect the family supplies. One of the best examples is at Bennet's Bar, Tollcross (walk 8), where it is called Jug and Bottle, so named, of course, after the vessels used to take home the chosen liquids. Other intact examples can be found at the Prestoungrange Gothenburg, Prestonpans (walk 19), where it is called Jug Bar; and the Harbour Bar, Kirkcaldy (walk 21).

Other characteristics of Scottish pubs

Brewery and Whisky Mirrors

Many Scottish (and Irish) bars are embellished with old mirrors, usually advertising long-vanished spirits and breweries/beers, as well as soft drinks and occasionally tobacco products. Some, like those at the Barony Bar (walk 3) are of truly epic size. Other mirrors can be seen at H P Mather's and the Bow Bar (walk 2), and Thomson's Bar (walk 12).

Water Taps on the Bar

Scotland is famous for whisky. Since whisky is the only spirit that can benefit from a little added water, a large numbers of counter tops had, and some still have, water taps. A few are still in working order, such as those at Bennet's

Water tap on the bar counter at Bennet's

Bar, Tollcross (walk 8) and Ryrie's Bar (walk 12). Ceramic jugs bearing whisky advertising are to be found on most Scottish bars for customers to add their own water.

CAMRA's National Inventory of Historic Pub Interiors

Preservation of historic pub interiors is a key issue for CAMRA. In 1997 CAMRA published its first *National Inventory of Pub Interiors of Outstanding Historic Interest*. The National Inventory of Historic Pub Interiors is published in two parts: Part One lists pubs whose interiors remain largely or wholly intact since before World War Two, whilst Part Two lists pubs whose interiors have been altered but which retain exceptional rooms or features of national historic importance. The Scottish regional inventory of historic pub interiors, published as *Scotland's True Heritage Pubs* list pubs on Parts One and Two of CAMRA's National Inventory of Historic Pub Interiors as well as other pubs which, although changed, still retain much of their historic layout and/or fittings. Where a pub in this guide is listed in the National Inventory of Historic Pub Interiors or in Scotland's True Heritage Pubs this information is included in the Pub Information box at the end of each route. For more information about CAMRA's project to save the UK's historic pub interiors visit www.heritagepubs.org.uk

Pounds, shillings and (dis)pense

Apologies for the groan-inducing title. At first glance, cask ale might seem hard to come by in some of the pubs in this guide: bar counters bristling with tall lager-style fonts, serving cryptically-named beers like 80/- seem worlds away from the handpumps serving Bitter that readers used to drinking in English pubs might expect.

The peculiar naming system for Scottish beers dates back to a 19th-century practice of stating the wholesale price for beer per barrel in shillings. The traditional, classic styles you will see are 60/- or Light, low in strength and so-called even when dark in colour; 70/- or Heavy; 80/- or Export; and the strong 90/- Wee Heavy, similar to a barley wine. For more on Scottish beers, see the beer styles section on pages 148-50

The Aitken founts at the Abbotsford

The Scottish dispense method

Scotland had, and in a few cases still retains, its own unique method for dispensing real ale: the tall fount (the 'u' is silent), through which the beer is raised by air pressure using a water engine (hydraulic pressure engine). In pubs still using the tall fount, the water engines have now been replaced by electric air compressors.

Introduced in the 1870s, the fount requires air pressures ranging from 12lb psi to as much as 40lb psi, depending upon the available mains pressure. The tap is opened and beer is served at the counter by 'pushing' the beer by air pressure, as compared to the English method of drawing it by suction using a beer-engine (hand-pump). It is an efficient way to produce a pint of real ale in prime condition, with an enticing, naturally produced creamy head.

The original system used a water engine. This unlikely device was introduced in Victorian times (1876) and was inspired by the cutting-edge technology of the time, the water closet cistern. Mains water was connected to a sealed, cast-iron chamber; as this chamber filled it compressed the air above the water until its pressure was sufficient to feed, through a non-return valve, into the dispense system's air supply.

When the chamber was full of water a float tripped a weighted lever that simultaneously cut off the water supply, opened a drain cock and opened a valve to allow more air to be drawn in. As the cistern emptied the float fell and reset this tripping mechanism, closing the air inlet and drain and opening the water inlet again – the whole cycle would repeat indefinitely while air was being used by the bar dispensers. If dispensing stopped, a diaphragm valve connected to the air system sensed when the system was up to full pressure and interrupted the float and lever system to hold the 'engine' in a static state, awaiting its next call to duty. One can only speculate how twenty-first century water companies would view such devices.

This once-common method of serving beer is, however, rarely used now but founts can still be found in service on Edinburgh bar counters. The Bow Bar (walk 2), Abbotsford Bar (walk 6), Athletic Arms (walk 11), Thomson's Bar (walk 12) and Bennet's Bar in Morningside (walk 15) all use Aitken founts.

As traditional Scottish founts are tall, have a tap at the top and look remarkably like lager and keg fonts, they have been replaced in many other pubs by the handpump, as the widely perceived correct method of serving real ale.

With thanks to *Roger Protz, Duncan McAra* and *Patrick O'Neill*

The Royal Edinburgh Military Tattoo

Edinburgh – Festival city

With a year-round calendar of events and festivals Edinburgh has become known as the world's Festival City. The most famous are of course the International and Fringe Festivals in August, but a plethora of other festivals and events mean that there's always something going on. A selection of events and festivals are listed below.

JANUARY:

Burns Night
25th January: various Burns Suppers, ceilidhs and other events take place around the city to celebrate the birthdate of Scotland's National Bard, Robert Burns.

MARCH:

Ceilidh Culture Festival
Last week of March to third week of April: annual traditional arts festival, which celebrates all aspects of the traditional arts from music and song to dance and storytelling.

APRIL:

Edinburgh International Science Festival
First two weeks of April: scientists and technologists share their passion with the public through a programme of engaging, interactive and accessible talks, workshops, shows and exhibitions.

Beltane Fire Festival
30th April: the Beltane Fire Festival is a revival of an ancient Celtic fertility festival: a unique and wild procession of fire, drumming and revelry, justifiably

Beltane May Queen

famous for its intensity and colour, held every year on Calton Hill.

MAY:

Imaginate Festival
Second week of May: theatre for children and young people.

JUNE:

Edinburgh International Film Festival
Third and fourth weeks of June: this twelve day festival presents film premiers, retrospectives on cinematic legends, personal talks and a plethora of industry events that attract audiences of over 55,000 each year.

Seven Hills Race
3rd Sunday in June: a fourteen mile race with no fixed course, taking in the summits of the Seven Hills of Edinburgh.

Scottish Real Ale Festival
Last weekend in June: CAMRA beer festival held at the Assembly Rooms on George Street, featuring the Champion Beer of Scotland competition. Beers from 30 Scottish breweries as well as breweries south of the border.

AUGUST:

Edinburgh Jazz & Blues Festival
First week of August: The best international musicians rub shoulders with top Scottish talent to present unique collaborations, world premieres and Scottish debuts – including the UK's largest jazz event, Jazz on A Summer's Day in Princes Street Gardens.

Edinburgh Art Festival
Last week of July to first week of September: The city's galleries, museums and visual art spaces combine to present the most exciting and intriguing of the modern and contemporary visual arts world.

Edinburgh Mela Festival
First weekend in August: An exciting celebration and exploration of the people, places and identities that reflect the diverse communities of the world.

Edinburgh Festival Fringe
Last three weeks of August: The largest arts festival in the world transforms Edinburgh with live theatre and comedy performances in the streets and across over 200 venues around the city.

Edinburgh Military Tattoo
Last three weeks of August: A unique blend of music, ceremony, entertainment and theatre set against magnificent Edinburgh Castle.

Edinburgh International Festival
Third week of July to first week of September: The finest in classical music, theatre, opera and dance gather to present one of the most innovative and accessible Festivals of the performing arts.

Edinburgh International Book Festival
Last two weeks of August: The largest book festival of its kind, with over 700 world-class writers and thinkers taking part in more than 800 events.

Edinburgh International Book Festival

OCTOBER:

International Storytelling Festival
Last week of October: Scotland's inspirational annual celebration of traditional and contemporary storytelling.

NOVEMBER:

St. Andrew's Day
30th November: various Edinburgh attractions offer free entry, including Edinburgh Castle, Edinburgh Zoo, the Scottish Parliament, Trinity House, Scottish Mining Museum, Craigmillar Castle and Linlithgow Palace. Other events include a free ceilidh at The Hub and firework display from Edinburgh Castle.

DECEMBER:

Edinburgh's Winter Wonderland
Last week of November to first week of January: over December an ice skating rink, fairground, the Edinburgh Wheel and market stalls spring up in Princes Street Gardens. Including the Traditional German Christmas Market on the Mound.

Edinburgh's Hogmanay
29th December to 2nd January – The largest New Year event in the world with five days of celebrations including the Night Afore ceilidh on George Street on the 30th, culminating in a massive New Year's Eve street party and winding down with events such as Edinburgh's Dogmanay dog sled racing in Holyrood Park and the Loony Dook where people brave the freezing waters of the Firth of Forth at South Queensferry on New Year's Day.

Edinburgh's Hogmanay street party

Edinburgh Old and New

top: **Ryrie's Bar Window**   bottom: **W. M. Mather's frontage**

Waverley Circuit

WALK INFORMATION

Start/Finish: Waverley Steps

Access: Trains to Waverley, buses to Waverley Bridge and Princes Street

Distance: 0.5 miles (0.8km)

Key attractions: Scott Monument, St. Andrew Square, General Register House

The pubs: Tiles, Café Royal, Guildford Arms

Links: to walks 2, 3, 6 and 8

This three pub hop is a good introduction to the city for the discerning drinker. It's a great route if you're in the city and pushed for time too, since it is by some distance the shortest walk in the book; in fact two of the pubs are literally next door to each other! It certainly doesn't lack quality for either the palate or the eyes however: all of the pubs reflect the superlative architecture of Edinburgh's New Town, the area of the city north of Princes Street. Indeed in the Café Royal you'll see some of the finest Victorian pub architecture in all Scotland. Don't expect to have these pubs to yourself though, so if you're keen to avoid the crowds I recommend you try and do this one early in the day or at least during the week when things are usually less hectic.

Start at the Tourist Information centre on Princes Street, at the top of Waverley Steps. (If you've arrived at Waverley station the steps are across the footbridge over platform 2, or if these look too daunting, take the road ramp which brings you out on Waverley Bridge and then turn right). Princes Street, the city's rather messy main shopping street stretches away to your left whilst towering above you stands the solid clock tower of what used to be the North British Hotel but is now the Balmoral,

Café Royal exterior with the red lobster above the entrance

Key

▪ ▪ ▪ ▪ ▪ Walk route

• • • • • • Detour

Tile section in the bar at the Café Royal

The Guildford

St Andrew Square

Melville Monument

General Register Office

General Register House

WEST REGISTER ST

LEITH ST

ROSE STREET

SOUTH ST ANDREW ST

SOUTH ST DAVID ST

MEUSE LANE

WATERLOO PLACE

Tourist Information

PRINCES STREET

Scott Monument

Royal Scottish Academy

National Gallery

THE MOUND

WAVERLEY BRIDGE

Waverley Station

NORTH BRIDGE

Waverley station's hotel. The station itself of course was named after the novel by Sir Walter Scott and nothing could demonstrate more strongly the high regard in which Edinburgh holds the famous author than the colossal Scott Monument a little way down the street. A 200-foot high masterpiece of Victorian Gothic extravagance, designed by George Meikle Kemp, it was completed in 1846, some 15 years after Scott's death. You can ascend to the top, with superb views in all directions for a small admission fee. It might enhance your appetite as you won't be walking very far horizontally!

Cross Princes Street and take South St. David Street directly opposite the Monument, which quickly brings you to the southwestern corner of St. Andrew Square. Rose Street (see walk 6), one of the five parallel roads of the early part of James Craig's eighteenth century New Town project runs away to your left but we turn right and walk along the southern part of the square. The tall column in the centre is the Melville Monument topped by a statute of Henry

Dundas, the Earl of Melville, a crony of William Pitt and by all accounts a rather dodgy 18th century politician. Some things don't change so much…

Just before you reach the far end of the square is the frontage of our first port of call,

Scott Monument

The sumptuous interior of Tiles

Tiles [1]. This is one of several notable pub conversions in the city in recent years, although in fact the atmosphere is more café bar than traditional pub. The building was formerly in the hands of the Prudential Insurance Co. and inside, the spacious bar lives up to its name, being completely tiled from floor to ceiling. Large windows, a remarkably high ceiling and enormous lamps form the character of the interior. Tiles offers a decent range of cask ales, with Edinburgh's signature beer, Caledonian Deuchars IPA – a deservedly popular modern-style straw coloured ale – a regular; but with up to three additional guests. Don't be put off by the modern keg-style founts. If you're here early you should be able to perch on one of the window-side high chairs and watch the world go by outside around the square; but there's also outside seating if you prefer.

Well, that's most of the walking done already! Come out of Tiles and head straight ahead across the main road to narrow West Register Street, and a few yards down look for the red lobster above a projecting black and white sign: you can't really miss the **Café Royal** [2]. The exterior is very elegant and as the name implies the place started life as a café in 1862; but it's the interior that sets this pub apart. Without a doubt it's one of the finest, if not the finest, pub interiors in Scotland, one of only very few listed at Grade A. For a full description I recommend you consult your copy of *Scotland's True Heritage Pubs*, but not to be missed are the six wonderful Doulton tiled murals, featuring innovators like Faraday, Watt and Stevenson; the marble floor and even more impressive ceiling; and the stunning island bar with an array of ornate brass light fittings. Choose a beer from a wide range – a couple of guests in addition to the regulars from the Caledonian brewery, kept well enough to earn a place in the *Good Beer Guide*; but at the very least also go and take a peek into the Oyster Bar, behind a walnut screen at the right hand end of the building. This is now an upmarket restaurant area, but it contains some excellent stained glass windows and a wonderful marble counter – not to be missed. The former upstairs bar which is also in the premier division architecturally (featured on the front cover of *Scotland's True Heritage Pubs* in its former livery) is now an upmarket cabaret-style suite currently known as the Voodoo Rooms, but you should be able to go up and have a look if you're keen. The entrance is round the corner to the left upon exit from the pub.

Coming out of the Café Royal you can almost fall into your next pub, the **Guildford Arms** [3] as it is quite literally next door! This handsome red sandstone building on a corner site is also architecturally interesting, notably for its Jacobean painted ceiling and pseudo Rococo cornices and freizes. However if it's a range of beers you're after then the Guildford exceeds expectations. There are

The elegant interior of the Café Royal

normally eight to choose from, with Scottish microbreweries well supported along with interesting imports from south of the border. Like the Café Royal there is a restaurant area here (it's upstairs) so if you're feeling peckish you should be able to find something that suits. Be warned again that the Guildford can get extremely busy especially at the weekend, no surprise given its central location, although service is usually efficient.

Coming out of the Guildford it's just a few yards walk back down to Princes Street, close to the junction with North Bridge. Pause to admire the magnificent General Register House immediately on your left – the oldest purpose-built archive repository still in use in Europe. It was designed by Robert Adam and first opened in 1789. Pub architecture devotees with time to spare might wish to detour a few yards further east, crossing with care over Leith Street and continuing ahead on Waterloo Place only for a few yards when you will come across the **Waterloo Buffet** 4 at No. 3, which at the foot of a handsome but plain three story stone terrace is a tiny and shallow bar which retains its century-old gantry. Otherwise, the big clock tower of the Balmoral should guide you easily back to your starting point in no time at all.

> LINK

The interior of the Guildford Arms

PUB INFORMATION

1 Tiles
1 St Andrew Sq, Edinburgh, EH2 2BD
0131 558 1507
Opening Hours: 11-11 (midnight Fri & Sat); 11-6 Sun

2 Café Royal
19 West Register St, Edinburgh, EH2 2AA
www.caferoyal.org.uk
0131 553 5080
Opening Hours: 11 (12.30 Sun)-11 (midnight Thu; 1am Fri & Sat)
CAMRA National Inventory (Part 2)

3 Guildford Arms
1-5 West Register St, Edinburgh, EH2 2AA
0131 556 4312
www.guildfordarms.com
Opening Hours: 11-11 (12 Fri & Sat); 12.30-11

TRY ALSO:

4 Waterloo Buffet
3 Waterloo Pl, Edinburgh, EH1 3BG
0131 556 7597
Opening Hours: 11-9 (1am Fri & Sat); 12-9 Sun
CAMRA National Inventory (Part 2)

> LINK Walks 2, 3, 6 and 8. Pick up the start of these routes at Waverley Steps.

Around the Castle

WALK INFORMATION

Start/Finish: Waverley Steps

Access: Trains to Waverley, buses to Waverley Bridge and Princes Street

Distance: 2.5 miles (4km)

Key attractions: Princes Street Gardens, Scott Monument, the Mound, St. Johns's Church

The pubs: H P Mather's Bar, Blue Blazer, Bow Bar

Links: to walks 1, 3, 4, 6 and 8

I'd rate this circuit for its length as one of the world's great urban walks for things to look at – fine buildings including Playfair's two great museums on the Mound, the lovely Princes Street gardens, some amazing vertical construction in Victoria Street, rounding off with the classic view down the Royal Mile. And all the while the iconic Edinburgh Castle towers above you. And we haven't forgotten that this is a pub book – the three pubs on this walk offer a good sample of Edinburgh's drinking scene, and there's every chance you'll come across some new or unusual beers.

Start at Waverley Steps, as per walk 1, and turn left to walk along Princes Street, crossing at the junction with Waverley Bridge. Steps lead down into the eastern part of Princes Street Gardens past the lovely floral display which is regularly changed. The area of the gardens were once occupied by a lake, the Nor' Loch, but by the 18th century this had become a putrid morass and residents of the city were pleased when it was drained. Pass under the Scott Monument (see walk 1) and walk along to a couple of celebrated Edinburgh architect

Edinburgh Castle

left: **The Scott Monument at night** right: **Ross Fountain**

William Playfair's finest buildings, the Royal Scottish Academy (1834) and the adjacent National Gallery (1848). They were built on the Mound, an artificial elevation constructed to improve access between the Old Town and a growing New Town to the north. Above you, the Castle Rock and the Castle itself dominate the scene as they

do throughout most of this walk; to your right of course is Princes Street, the southernmost of William Craig's parallel New Town avenues, certainly the best known and undoubtedly the ugliest thanks to some thoughtless postwar developments. By the time you read this the

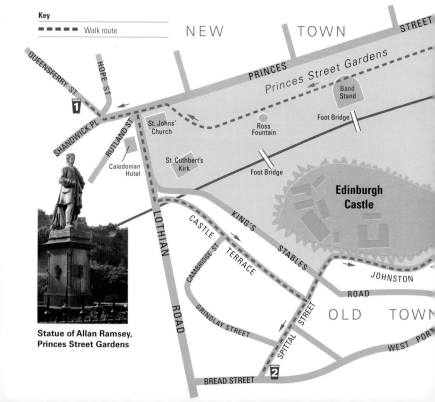

Key

▬ ▬ ▬ ▬ ▬ Walk route

NEW TOWN STREET

QUEENSFERRY ST

HOPE ST

1

SHANDWICK PL

RUTLAND ST

St. Johns' Church

Caledonian Hotel

St. Cuthbert's Kirk

PRINCES

Princes Street Gardens

Ross Fountain

Band Stand

Foot Bridge

Foot Bridge

Edinburgh Castle

LOTHIAN ROAD

CASTLE

CAMBRIDGE ST

TERRACE

KING'S

STABLES

JOHNSTON ROAD

GRINDLAY STREET

SPITTAL STREET

OLD TOWN

WEST PORT

BREAD STREET

2

Statue of Allan Ramsey, Princes Street Gardens

construction of the tram system along the length of Princes Street will be well under way and this may herald some welcome improvements.

Crossing the Mound re-enter the gardens, strolling past the bandstand, with fine views up to the Castle. You can get very close to the bottom of the Castle Crag further west when a footbridge crosses the railway (cut in 1846) and a path leads up to King's Stables Road. Disregard this for now however and head instead past the ornate iron Ross Fountain and the handsome St. Cuthbert's Kirk with its pretty steeple and climb up towards St. John's Church above it where there is a little Fairtrade shop and cafe which might appeal before the day's drinking begins. Our first pub is now close by: reaching Princes Street cross onto the northern side and

H P Mather's Bar

bearing left cross over Hope Street and then in front of you slightly to your right on Queensferry Street is **H P Mather's Bar 1**. Arriving here earlier in the day is the best time to appreciate the internal layout of this attractive bar. It's a handsome single room dominated by the attractive back gantry and plenty of bar mirrors, presided over by a good quality ceiling and frieze. The real ales here are from the Caledonian brewery a mile away. Warning: If

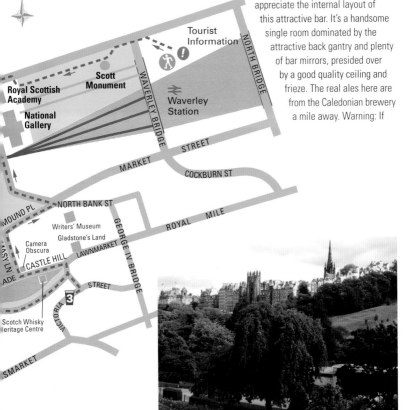

Princes Street Gardens

Royal Scottish Academy

enthusiasts may be interested to know that the imposing Caledonian Hotel is all that remains of the Princes Street terminal station (and the goods terminus south of it) of the Caledonian railway, which was closed in the mid-1960s and demolished some years later. Much of the land once occupied by the train sheds and tracks is now the new financial centre of the city, hence the cluster of brash modern buildings along the Lothian Road.

you're meeting someone here be aware, to avoid confusion, that there is another *Mather's Bar*, on Broughton Street half a mile away.

Leaving the pub return to the southern side of Princes Street and head southwards along the busy Lothian Road. Across the street, railway

Take Castle Terrace which leads off on the left after about 150 yards and follow this road with excellent views of the Castle towering above you. Between 9 and 2 every Saturday this street

GRASSMARKET'S ORIGINS

The Grassmarket's origins lie with it being in a valley, which meant it was easier for livestock and carts to access rather than having to negotiate the steep slope up to the Old Town. For this reason the area was probably used as a market from the 1300s, although recently archaeological finds suggest it has been used by man as far back as the Middle Bronze Age, around 1400BC. It took its name from farmers selling hay, corn and seed; later it became a business centre, with printers, tanners, brewers, tobacconists, corn merchants and candlemakers trading. A central feature of the Grassmarket is the Bow Well built in 1681 as the first piped outlet of running water in Edinburgh. The Grassmarket had a darker side too: next to the well is the Covenanter's memorial, a reminder of the Grassmarket's place in the history of Edinburgh as the site of the city's gallows; which was the scene of many hangings, and the infamous Porteous riot in 1736, when John Porteous, the brutal Captain of the Town Guard, was taken from prison and lynched by a mob in the Grassmarket. Executions ceased here in 1784, when James Andrews became the last person to be hanged in the Grassmarket – for robbery.

Most of the buildings in the Grassmarket date from the 1800's, following a period of improvement in the Old Town. Several buildings from the 1700's survive on the northern and eastern sides most notably the *White Hart Inn*. In the 19th century, the area spiralled into squalor and poverty. But like much of old Edinburgh the 20th century has seen the area rehabilitated and transformed into something of a tourist mecca.

Grassmarket today

left: **The landmark spire of The Hub** right: **A good array of beers at the Blue Blazer**

is occupied by the excellent Edinburgh Farmers' Market with stalls selling all manner of fresh seasonal goods, including bottled beers from both Black Isle and Stewart breweries.

At the end of this street bear right at the T junction into Spittal Street and walk along to its junction with Bread Street where on the corner you will find the **Blue Blazer** 2. This is an attractive and convivial city pub, which is deservedly popular. A main room hosts the servery, and a smaller one leads off, both with a few nooks and corners offering some intimacy despite the fact that it's often busy. It offers one of the best beer ranges in the city centre – there are eight handpumps dispensing a changing range of guest beers alongside regulars from the nearby Stewart brewery, and the ever-popular Cairngorm Trade Winds.

Retrace your steps to the junction with Castle Terrace, but this time continue straight ahead, again with the castle dominating the view, into Johnston Terrace. This is a pleasant walk along a road which climbs gently but steadily up into the Old Town. To your right a wide view opens up across the south of the city with George Heriot School

prominent in the near distance. Below you but well hidden is the Grassmarket (see box) which if you have the time and energy is well worth a detour although none of its pubs quite meet the exacting standards to merit inclusion in this guide! Access it either down the Patrick Geddes Steps (also known as Castle Wynd South) on the right along here, or walk down Victoria Street beyond the Bow Bar (easier but less dramatic, see below).

Just before Johnson Terrace merges into Castle Hill by The Hub a small alleyway leads off to the right and brings you in about 20 yards to a narrow terrace where you are looking down onto

St. John's Church from Queensferry Street

left: **St. Cuthbert's Kirk**   right: **Striking vertical development in West Bow**

a street below you. Don't worry if you miss it because you can take the wider lane, Upper Bow, beyond it, immediately short of the junction with Castle Hill. Below you is Victoria Street, but the effect of one set of high buildings perched on another is quite sublime and the only enhanced by being able to look down on our next pub, the very attractive **Bow Bar 3**. To reach it take the steps downwards at the end of Upper Bow or if you prefer continue along the terrace and at the end double back down Victoria Street. The Bow Bar is an excellent example of a top-quality refurbishment of what used to be a rundown tenement bar, and in a way is a metaphor for the regeneration of Edinburgh's Old Town. All the fixings inside including the excellent back gantry have been brought from elsewhere but the effect is very satisfying and the pub is deservedly popular. There are up to eight well-kept ales most of which are rotating guest beers from anywhere in Britain. You can hardly fail to notice the excellent range of single malt whiskies. As you leave the Bow Bar cheese

enthusiasts may wish to drop into I J Mellis's cheesemongers across the street: there are other branches of this excellent business in Stockbridge and Morningside.

Retrace your steps to the junction of Johnston Terrace and Castle Hill bearing left if you wish to visit the Castle itself. 〉**LINK 1**〈

There are several options to return to Waverley station. Perhaps the best is to reverse the first part of walk 4 by turning up Castle Hill and taking Ramsey Lane, the first turning on the right, which quickly leads you down to the Mound. 〉**LINK 2**〈

If it's food you need, you could try the *Castle Arms* on Johnston Terrace (see walk 4) or pick up walk 4 in the correct direction and head down either to the *Malt Shovel* or walk further down the Royal Mile and call in at the *Halfway House* in Fleshmarket Close.

PUB INFORMATION

1 H P Mather's Bar
1 Queensferry St, Edinburgh,
EH2 4PA
0131 225 3549
Opening Hours: 11-midnight (1am Fri & Sat); 12.30-11 Sun
CAMRA National Inventory (Part 2)

2 Blue Blazer
2 Spittal St, Edinburgh, EH3 9DX
0131 229 5030
Opening Hours: 11(12.30 Sun)-1am

3 Bow Bar
80 West Bow, Edinburgh, EH1 2HH
0131 226 7667
Opening Hours: 12-11.30; 12.30-11 Sun

〉**LINK 1**〈 Walk 4, **Best of the Royal Mile – top** (page 33). Pick up the start of walk 4 at the Castle Esplanade.

〉**LINK 2**〈 Walks 1, 3, 6 & 8. Continue right along Princes Street to Waverley Steps to pick up the start of these routes.

Over Calton Hill to Broughton

WALK INFORMATION

Start/Finish: Waverley Steps

Access: Trains to Waverley, buses to Waverley Bridge and Princes Street

Distance: 1.5 miles (2.5km)

Key attractions: Calton Hill, Nelson Monument, National Monument, City Observatory

The pubs: Cask & Barrel, Barony Bar

Links: to walk 7

Along with the Castle Rock itself, Calton Hill is the nearest of Edinburgh's 'seven hills' to the city centre, and the views are worth the climb. Dominating the view east along Princes Street, the gorse-strewn volcanic outcrop with its eclectic and iconic collection of buildings on the summit has no comparison in any other British city. As a pub walk it's absolutely ideal: a short but exhilarating climb, great views, an optional coffee shop at the bottom, then into one of the architecturally classy inner suburbs for a pint or two. And it can all be done in a couple of hours if need be.

Start as usual at the Scott Monument or the Tourist Office at the top of Waverley Steps. Cross Princes Street to the side with all the shops, and the first part is simplicity itself: using the Nelson Monument (the tall tower on the hilltop) as your navigation, simply walk in a straight line towards it. You'll pass Robert Adam's Register House on your left just before crossing Leith Street which heads downhill towards the port. Walk along Waterloo Place, and just before you get to the gargantuan Art Deco pile of St.

Andrew's House on the opposite side of the street, look for some steps heading up to the hill on your left. If you miss them, or if you prefer a longer slope to a steep set of steps, there's an alternative access at the far end of St. Andrew's House by a lay-by and driveway – (in this case double sharply back towards the hilltop at the end of the slope).

Turn right up another flight of steps to head up towards the summit, passing the distinctly Grecian-looking columnar monument to the

The striking clock tower of the Balmoral

philosopher Dugald Stewart on the way. On your right as you climb (left of course if you came via the sloping alternative route) is a great view across to the grassy slopes of Holyrood Park culminating abruptly in the extinct volcano of Arthur's Seat. Left of the summit as you look are the remains of old lava flows, whilst right, closer to the city, the sloping reddish volcanic outcrop is Salisbury Crags. This is an ancient sill, a horizontal intrusion of molten rock squeezed between layers of sedimentary rock. It was this rock, known to quarrymen as whinstone, which was used for the paving setts that cobbled the streets of Edinburgh.

By now you should have arrived at the Nelson Monument on top of Calton Hill. Designed by Robert Bergen in the shape of an upturned telescope,

The Cask & Barrel

Key

▪ ▪ ▪ ▪ ▪ Walk route

● ● ● ● ● ● ● Alternative walk route

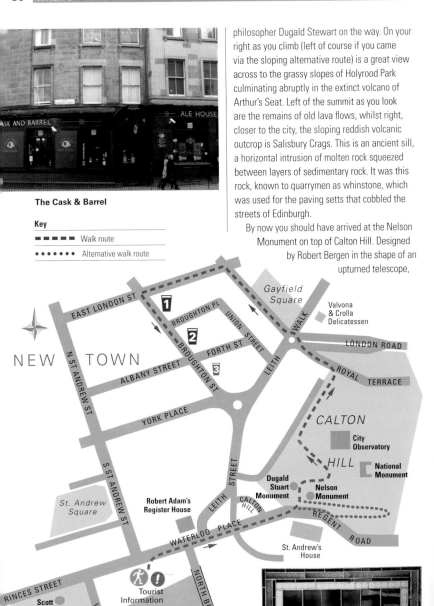

Tile detail from Barony Bar

and completed in 1816 this is one of Edinburgh's landmark buildings, and for an admission charge it's possible to ascend to the rather exposed viewing platform for even better views. The time ball on the top was installed to signal the time to ships in Leith harbour and is dropped at 1pm every day, at the same time as the One O'Clock Gun from Edinburgh Castle.

The attractive frontage of the Barony Bar

From the terrace around the Nelson Monument, you can see straight down Princes Street whilst closer to hand is a motley but impressive range of architecture. Probably the most bizarre is the unfinished National Monument designed by the great architect William Playfair (1790-1857) as a replica of the Parthenon in Athens. Unfortunately in an early example of a modern malaise the money ran out; and 'Edinburgh's Disgrace' as it became known remains unfinished. Some have unkindly compared this to the budgeting problems of the new Scottish Parliament building! Playfair also built the nearby City Observatory in 1818 based on another Athenian building, the Temple of the Winds.

Heading off the hill we are aiming north, so either walk down to the Dugald Stewart Monument and take the curving path to the right from it, or cut across past the near side of the observatory and with unwelcome views down to the grim '60s St. James shopping centre below, head for the lower (stepped) path at the boundary of the hill leading steadily down and bringing you off the hill at

the north entrance on Royal Terrace, yet again the work of Playfair. The gardens ahead lead quite steeply down to the London Road where there is a further collection of handsome buildings, but we can simply turn left and walk down to join the road in fifty yards just short of the busy junction of the top of the Leith Walk. We are aiming for Gayfield Square across the road, but if you have time you may wish to entertain a brief interlude at Valvona & Crolla, the famous Edinburgh institution a short distance down the hill on your right (19 Elm Row, set back a little from the main road). This Italian family-run delicatessen is probably Scotland's most famous, and has been here since the 1930's. There is a small cafe at the rear serving a range of food from light bites to substantial meals.

Cross Leith Walk and follow Gayfield Square straight down until you join East London Street by a primary school. Turn left and in about 250 yds right on the corner is the **Cask & Barrel** . A spacious alehouse at the bottom of a traditional tenement block, the interior is comfortable

The unfinshed National Monument, Calton Hill

W. M. Mather's

and pubby with the impressive horseshoe bar dominating but with plenty of standing and sitting space around it. Note the fine cornice and the collection of brewery mirrors, still commonplace in a city which once had a plethora of breweries. One warning: if you're averse to pub TVs there's little escape here – I lost count at seven last time I was in, although mercifully they're not always switched on. It's the ale here in this *Good Beer Guide* regular which impresses the most, however: up to nine available, with changing guests alongside old favourites like Caledonian Deuchars IPA and Harviestoun Bitter & Twisted. Meals are served at lunchtime with bar snacks at other times.

Leaving the Cask & Barrel, turn left up the hill along Broughton Street and a very short distance up (No. 81) is the second pub on this walk, the **Barony Bar 2**. This handsome hansome tenement pub with its pleasing wooden frontage has a late Victorian internal scheme and well deserves its place in *Scotland's True Heritage Pubs*. Although it has been opened out internally, much

survives from the late Victorian refit, notably the solid bar counter and back gantry, some wonderful tiled pictures and a couple of huge whisky mirrors. The pub also features in the *2010 Good Beer Guide* and offers a range of guest beers as well as familiar faces like Deuchars IPA and Black Sheep Best Bitter. Moreover, food is available here until 10pm (7 on Sunday). **LINK**

It's really not far at all back into the city centre, but a No. 8 bus will take the strain if you wish.

If you want to try another pub, **W. M. Mather's 3** bar is a short walk up from the Barony and offers up to four ales in an attractive building with open fires, and some fine wood and tile work.

LINK Walk 7 **Squares and Crescents of the New Town** (page 51) There are links by bus to several routes; but on foot, cross the road from the Barony Bar and take Barony Street almost opposite. Cut through the mews at the end to Dublin Street, and cross over into Dublin Meuse [sic]. Here is the *Star Bar*, and you can reverse walk 7 from here.

PUB INFORMATION

1 Cask & Barrel
115 Broughton St, Edinburgh,
EH1 3RZ
0131 556 3132
www.caskandbarrel.co.uk
Opening Hours: 11 (12.30 Sun)-
12.30am (1am Thu-Sat)

2 Barony Bar
81-85 Broughton St, Edinburgh,
EH1 3RJ
0131 558 2874
Opening Hours: 11 (12.30 Sun)-
midnight (1am Fri & Sat)
CAMRA National Inventory (Part 2)

TRY ALSO:

3 W. M. Mather's
25 Broughton St, Edinburgh,
EH1 3JU
0131 556 6754
Opening Hours: 11-midnight
(12.30am Fri & Sat); 12.30-11 Sun

Best of the Royal Mile – the Castle

WALK INFORMATION

Start: Castle Esplanade

Finish: The Tron

Access: Buses 23, 27, 41 and 45 to the Lawnmarket

Distance: 0.7 miles (1.1 km)

Key attractions: Edinburgh Castle, Camera Obscura, Scotch Whisky Heritage Centre, Gladstone's Land Museum, St. Giles Cathedral, Real Mary King's Close

The pubs: Castle Arms, Jolly Judge, Malt Shovel, Halfway House

Links: to walk 1, 2, 5, 8, and 13

The unique topography of Edinburgh's Old Town means that in practice the only way to really appreciate it is on foot. Until the eighteenth century this was the full extent of the city, and such was the competition for space that the housing densities were among Europe's highest, with the commensurate squalor and misery. Until relatively recently this was still an area with plenty of problems, although today the buildings have been restored and it's thronged with tourists for much of the year. This walk is full of interest all the way and if you combine this walk with the lower Royal Mile route (walk 5) you'll have to be self disciplined to reach the last pub before closing time, there is so much to see. Beer-wise, the last two pubs, particularly the Halfway House, offer the best beer range. Don't miss these out if you aren't intending to call at all four.

🚶 Start on Castle Esplanade outside the entrance to Edinburgh Castle. Buses 23, 27 and 45 will carry you the short distance up from the Mound (or 41 from Waverley Bridge) to the foot of the Lawnmarket by *Deacon Brodie's Tavern*. If you are visiting or have visited the Castle itself you'll probably want a far more detailed guide than the short summary provided

Ramsey Garden, the Camera Obscura and the Hub from Castle Esplanade

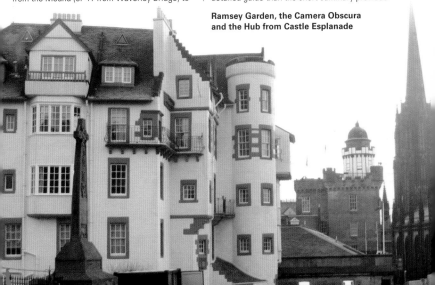

here (see box). Views are excellent all round, as you'd expect, although maybe not as good as those from Calton Hill where there isn't a castle in the way!

Facing away from the Castle and heading down the sloping whaleback ridge which was the 'tail' on which the early city developed, note especially the distinctive Art Nouveau houses of Ramsey Garden to your left. It's worth detouring briefly down Ramsay Lane (1st left, by the Camera Obscura) and left again past a row of 18th-century houses to look at the creation of Patrick Geddes, who many regard as the father of town planning. It was he who was a driving force behind the late 19th century revival of this part of the Old Town. His vision was of a tightly-knit academic community housing professors, with the surrounding tenements being restored as student living quarters. Today these flats with their superb views over the city and the Firth of Forth are some of the most desirable properties in the Old Town.

Back at the top of Ramsey Lane the Out-look Tower which houses the Camera Obscura (a system of mirrors and lenses project images onto a viewing table) is well worth a visit. There's also a display of holograms and other optical illusions, and panoramic views from the gallery at the top. Across the street is the Scotch Whisky Heritage Centre, whilst a little distance along a curious low building now housing the Edinburgh Weaving Company was originally the Castle Hill reservoir. Built in 1851 it supplied water to Princes Street; in turn the reservoir was fed by springs in the nearby Pentland Hills. Beyond here the Royal Mile opens out before you. Despite the tourists and all the associated tartan tat, this still remains one of Britain's finest streets. The first really noticeable building is the huge 75m spire of the former St. John's Kirk at the corner with Johnson Terrace, now known as The Hub. It actually started life as the Victoria Hall for the established Church General Assembly in 1844. It does contain a worthwhile café if you're not yet ready for beer. Talking of which, swinging round to the right at the Hub brings you onto Johnston Terrace, and a few doors along at No. 6 is the **Castle Arms** 🗍. It's an interesting place on account of the amazing topography here: at the rear of the place the land drops like a stone into West Bow and the Grassmarket (see walk 2);

Gladstone's Land

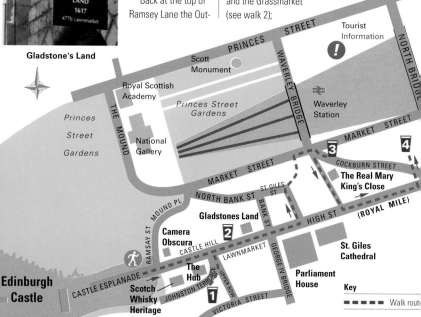

Castle Arms

a lower bar gives access to a terrace with views down. The main bar is plain, part bistro, but offers Caledonian 80 and Deuchars IPA; and if you're lucky, at busier times, a guest or two. Food

is available throughout the day. >LINK 1<

Back on the Royal Mile, a little further down on the left, with its distinctive street level arcade, is Gladstone's Land (or tenement) a property which has been restored by the National Trust for Scotland as a typical 17th century merchant's house. This remarkable building dates from the 1550s and has been in continuous use ever since. It's named for Thomas Gledstane, the merchant who bought and renovated the property around 1615. Above the entrance is a golden 'gled', an eagle-like bird from the Highlands used to identify the house in the days before street addresses. There is an admission charge but if you like your

EDINBURGH CASTLE

Edinburgh Castle is built on Castle Crag, the remains of a long extinct volcano, and has a long history having been extended incrementally since Norman times. Then of course it was only one of many royal castles at a time when Edinburgh was not the capital settlement. The earliest surviving building, a little chapel, was probably built by King David I (1124-53) in memory of his mother Queen Margaret, later Saint Margaret. Her representation appears on the left side of the crest of the City of Edinburgh, and South Queensferry was named after her, as she established a pilgrims' ferry there.

Like Dunbar the castle fell into English hands on several occasions before things settled down a little and during the reign of James III (1460-88), Edinburgh emerged as the capital city. About this time the castle was replanned.

After the abdication of Mary Queen of Scots as a result of a revolt following her marriage to James Hepburn, Earl of Bothwell in 1567, the castle underwent the 'Lang siege' This came about because the keeper of the castle, Sir William Kirkcaldy, remained loyal to her. However after over a year of stalemate the castle was eventually bombarded and reduced to rubble. Kirkcaldy was hanged for treason.

The rebuilt castle was less of a royal residence and after the union, it was Cromwell's creation of a permanent standing army, his 'New Model Army', that was to transform the castle into a garrison fortress. King Charles I was the last king

to stay overnight in the castle – on the eve of his coronation as King of Scots in 1633. But just as the castle underwent transformation from palace to garrison, with political stability it assumed more of a visitor attraction, bolstered in 1818 when Walter Scott, the famous novelist, together with the Governor of the castle, broke down the doors to the Crown Room to rediscover the Honours of Scotland which had been locked away after the 1707 Treaty of Union. The Honours were almost immediately placed on public display and people flocked to the castle to view them. So although the castle is still technically an Army HQ today the main garrison left for their new suburban barracks in 1923.

The castle today is home to the Scottish Crown Jewels (the Honours) and the Stone of Destiny. The latter was returned to Edinburgh Castle from Westminster Abbey in 1996 although its original resting place was at Scone Palace which would have perhaps been a more appropriate destination. Also at the castle today is the Scottish National War Memorial and the famous One O'Clock Gun, which is fired daily at 1pm, faithful to Mons Meg, the giant 15th century siege gun which although defunct since 1681 was first fired at 1pm.

history it's atmospheric, informative and interesting. This stretch of the Royal Mile is known as the Lawnmarket, but the name derives from the fine linen cloth that was once sold here rather than any greenery. Almost next door to Gladstone's Land, in fact just back up the hill a few yards, identifiable by the sign over the pend to James Court is the **Jolly Judge 2**. The narrow entry and the subterranean location raise expectations, although somehow the smart and brightly lit interior with carpets and rendered walls don't seem to make the most of the potential for cosiness and uniqueness. Despite that it's worth a visit not least for the beers – a

The Jolly Judge

couple of changing ales on handpump, and (a recent innovation) traditional cider. It can get packed in season, and empty in winter when the trippers aren't around in the evening, so it may close early. Bar lunches are available but no evening food.

Returning to street level continue down the Lawnmarket and over the junction by the *Deacon Brodie* pub. The view ahead is dominated by St. Giles Cathedral, or more properly the High Kirk of Edinburgh. It has evolved piecemeal since the 12th century with the distinctive crown spire being added in the late 15th century. Take the next turning left, Giles Street, although if

THE OLD TOWN

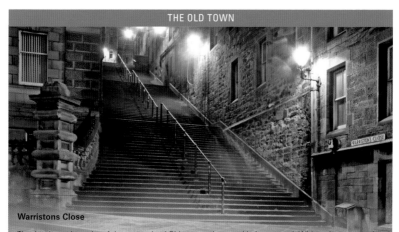

Warristons Close

The density and squalor of the constrained Old Town led to pressure from the wealthy classes for an escape into the potentially attractive areas north and south. The draining of the Nor'Loch (now occupied by Princes Street gardens) and the start of construction in the New Town, in around 1765, heralded the beginning of this process, which continued for well over a century. The increased divisions between rich and poor and gave Edinburgh two distinctly separate faces. On the one hand Edinburgh was dubbed the 'Athens of The North' during the period of Enlightenment, but in the Old Town people were still living in appalling conditions with outbreaks of diseases like Cholera, not to mention serious crime rates. Families were living, sometimes ten to a room,

above and below ground. Without investment the high-rise buildings (some over ten stories high) were left to fall into a state of increasing decay and some collapsed under their own weight, like one on the High Street which became known as the Heave Awa Hoose, after a young lad was rescued from the rubble after crying out "Heave awa' lads, I'm no deid yet".

A public outcry led to legislation in the form of The Act of Improvement (1867), giving the Municipality powers to tear down any building that was considered unsafe. The flight of the middle classes to the suburbs continued apace however, and the Old Town – centred upon the Royal Mile – remained an unfashionable place to live until comparatively recently.

you're either pushed for time or not keen on steps you can avoid the detour by continuing straight ahead and picking up the route again at the top of Advocates Close a hundred yards further along. (In this case you can visit the Malt Shovel if you wish via Cockburn Street.)

At the foot of Giles Street where the road turns left bear right into what looks like a cul-de-sac, and descend the steep News Steps ahead, named after the printing works of the Evening News which at one time was situated close by. Here there is a fine view over Princes Street to the gothic Scott Monument, and Calton Hill, crowned with the Nelson Monument and its unfinished replica of the Parthenon (walk 3). At the bottom turn right and then right again into Cockburn Street. This fine Victorian avenue was built around 1860 to improve access to Waverley station, dissecting several of the closes and slums which ran down from the Old Town. A short distance up on the opposite side is the **Malt Shovel** [3]. Wide, occupying at least two former houses, and shallow, what you see through the large clear windows is what you get. The lower room adjacent the bar with its good back gantry has a pleasant ambience with wooden floors and a (fake) fireplace. A couple of old brewery mirrors, including a fine one from Melville's Boroughloch brewery, adorn the walls. These mirrors are a common sight in Edinburgh pubs, no surprise given the number of former breweries in the city. Four steps lead into an upper room. There are four ales available, Caledonian 80 and Deuchars IPA as regulars, and two rotating guests. Live evening music sessions take place on Tuesday (jazz) and Thursday (folk). You'll get something to eat here until around 6pm.

Returning to the foot of Cockburn Street turn sharp left into Advocates Close. This is actually named after a former Lord Advocate, Sir James Stewart, and is one of the most atmospheric of the closes, and well lit at night.

While you're getting your breath back at the top of Advocates Close, you've time to admire the High Kirk of St. Giles (see box) and the Parliament Square which surrounds this substantial building. Behind the cathedral is Parliament House, home of the Scottish Parliament from 1640 until its

ST. GILES KIRK

As the parish church for the Old Town, St. Giles evolved incrementally from the 12th century onwards with the usual mixture of styles, although it is a 15th century building in the main. What you see today contains features of mediaeval Gothic and Renaissance architecture. The most notable external feature is the Crown Spire on the tower, added in the late 1400's. St. Giles' also has a fine collection of stained glass windows, dating from Victorian times in a broad range of traditional and contemporary designs. Perhaps the most famous minister here was John Knox (see walk 5) who served from 1559 until 1572.

During the reformation the interior of the church was partitioned, allowing the building to be used for a wide range of purposes. These included police and fire stations, a school and even a coal store! The Scottish guillotine, the "Maiden", was housed here, close to the Tolbooth prison (see below). The General Assembly of the Church of Scotland met in the building, as did the Parliament and the Town Council.

As a Presbyterian place of worship the cathedral's more correct title is the "High Kirk of Edinburgh", although this name has never stuck. Outside, the heart-shaped design set into the pavement marks the entrance to the Tolbooth. Originally established as the name implies, to collect tolls, it later became a prison with a scaffold for hanging criminals (and others) and the heads of the more famous victims would be displayed on spikes in the face of the building. Walter Scott immortalised the Tolbooth in his 'Heart of Midlothian' and the rest is, well, history. Just whence the tradition of spitting into the Heart derives is unclear, some say it brings luck, I prefer to think they are Hibs fans... The Tolbooth was demolished in 1817.

union with England's in 1707. The building was completed in 1639 but in the early 19th century the old building was refaced and surrounded by open arcades to fit in with the redevelopment taking place all around. The Great Hall, where the parliament met, had walls lined with rich tapestries and a huge arched oak roof spanning its 50 foot width. Parliament House is now used by silks practicing in the adjacent Courts.

Across the street is the City Chambers, built in 1753 as the Royal Exchange. Houses, several stories high, were decapitated and the lower sections were used as the foundations for the new development. These well-preserved subterranean labyrinths which have the reputation of being one of the most haunted places in Scotland are now part of one of Edinburgh's most popular visitor attractions, the Real Mary King's Close. Entry here is only possible with an organised tour. You're probably ready for another pint by now, especially if you go round, so with the attractive steeple of the Tron Kirk in front of you, look out for Fleshmarket Close on your left just before major road junction ahead. ▶LINK 2◀ The first section of this narrow entry slopes down to join the top of Cockburn Street, but across the road becomes a steep flight of steps with a welcome handrail, leading down to the **Halfway House** 4 .

This atmospheric little pub is something of an Edinburgh institution, and on account of its menu of well-kept beers is a firm favourite of the local branch of CAMRA, whose awards are displayed on the walls along with much railwayana. The

A jazz session in the Malt Shovel

limited space inside is well used, and there are several intimate little spaces to hole up and enjoy a pint. It's often busy but given its size it's surprising how often you can find a wee space to squeeze in! The beer range varies but the emphasis on the four handpumps is firmly on Scottish microbreweries: often a particular brewery is featured with several of their beers. Good and reasonably priced food is available all day.

You can continue straight onto walk 5, the bottom end of the Royal Mile, if you've the stamina ▶LINK 3◀ ; or to return to the city centre, simply walk down the remaining steps and in one minute you're at the Market Street entrance to Waverley station. Enter here and you can cut through to Princes Street by taking the footbridge across the station. ▶LINK 4◀

PUB INFORMATION

1 Castle Arms
6 Johnston Terr, Edinburgh,
EH1 2PW
0131 225 7432
www.castlearmsedinburgh.co.uk
Opening Hours: 11-midnight

2 Jolly Judge
7 James Ct, Lawnmarket, Edinburgh, EH1 2PB
0131 225 2669
www.jollyjudge.co.uk
Opening Hours: 12 (12.30 Sun)-11 (midnight Fri & Sat)

3 Malt Shovel
11/15 Cockburn St, Edinburgh,
EH1 1BP
0131 225 6843
Opening Hours: 11-midnight
(1am Fri & Sat); 12.30pm-11pm Sun

4 Halfway House
24 Fleshmarket Cl, Edinburgh,
EH1 1BX
0131 225 7101
www.halfwayhouse-edinburgh.com
Opening Hours: 11 (12.30 Sun)-midnight (1am Fri & Sat)

▶LINK 1◀ Walk 2 **Around the Castle** (page 23) Join the last part of the route to the Bow Bar; or walk down Johnston Terrace and reverse the rest of the route.

▶LINK 2◀ Walk 8 **Via the Meadows to Tollcross** (page 55) Join the first section of the route at Hunter Square, at the top of Fleshmarket Close.

▶LINK 2◀ Walk 13 **Into the Southside** (page 75) From The Tron Kirk walk or take a bus via South Bridge to Nicholson Square (0.25 miles).

▶LINK 3◀ Walk 5 **Best of the Royal Mile – Holyrood** (page 39) Return up the stairs to the Royal Mile and the Tron Kirk by Hunter Square in front of you.

▶LINK 4◀ Walk 1 **Waverley Circuit** (page 19) Pick up the start of this circuit from the station.

Best of the Royal Mile – Holyrood

Start: Tron Kirk, junction High Street and North Bridge

Finish: Regent Road

Access: Buses 29, 31, 33 and 37 from Princes Street

Distance: 1 mile (1.6km)

Key attractions: John Knox House, Canongate Kirk, Holyrood Abbey and Palace of Holyrood, Scottish Parliament buildings, Our Dynamic Earth (see www. dynamicearth.co.uk)

The pubs: The Mitre, Tass, Tolbooth Tavern, Regent

Links: to walk 3

Picking up where the previous route left off, you'll continue down the Royal Mile, with the volume of tourists tailing off, as you head down into the Canongate, once a separate burgh. Although the magnificent baroque palace of Holyrood is the key attraction, there is of course plenty more to see, and numerous closes to wander into and explore if you have extra time. Once again readers with a keen interest in the history of the city and of the old town in particular will be well advised to equip themselves with more detailed guides to the area, whilst relying upon this one to take you to the best of the watering holes.

The Tolbooth Tavern

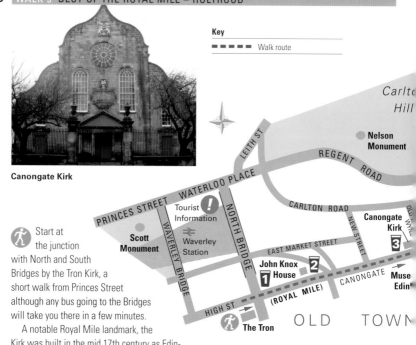

Canongate Kirk

Key
■ ■ ■ ■ ■ Walk route

Start at the junction with North and South Bridges by the Tron Kirk, a short walk from Princes Street although any bus going to the Bridges will take you there in a few minutes.

A notable Royal Mile landmark, the Kirk was built in the mid 17th century as Edinburgh's principal parish church after King Charles I elevated St. Giles into a cathedral. Remarkably the steeple is almost 200 years younger, dating from 1828. The name 'Tron' comes from the salt-tron, a public weighing beam which once stood outside. The church hasn't been used for worship for over half a century. In 1974 excavations revealed an old street, Marlin's Wynd, buried under the foundations and these are still visible in the building (which is intermittently used as a visitor centre) today. A short distance down from the Tron on the opposite side is **The Mitre 1**, with its attractive early 19th century stone frontage. It's quite a handsome place inside too, with a good back gantry and a large Campbell's brewery mirror on the wall. Campbell's Argyle brewery

Statue of poet Robert Fergusson outside Canongate Kirk

stood nearby in Chambers Street and was one of the city's oldest brewing firms. During the tourist season of course the place gets busy due to its location, but with two beers from Caledonian and two rotating guest beers there's at least a decent range of drinks to choose from. Food is available throughout the day and a large area to the back of the pub is set aside for that purpose.

Continuing down the hill it's the quaint and uneven John Knox House which stands out, but before you get there lookout on the left for Paisley Close and the inscription above the pend "Heave Awa' Chaps I'm No' Dead Yet" (see box, walk 4). The Celtic Craft Centre is down here too, and just beyond in Chalmers Close are two of the best cafes on the Royal Mile: Carrubbers café and Forsyth's tea room. Further down the close is the reconstructed Trinity College church, now a brass rubbing centre.

John Knox House, on your left, is an interesting building dating back to 1490; and reputed to have been the manse occupied by the great protestant reformer when he was minister at St. Giles Kirk in the mid 16th century.

A little further down at the traffic lights by the junction with Jeffrey Street, and currently

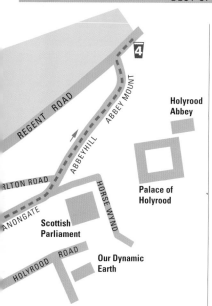

4

REGENT ROAD

ABBEY MOUNT

ABBEYHILL

?LTON ROAD

?RLTON ROAD

ANONGATE

Holyrood
Abbey

HORSE WYND

**Palace of
Holyrood**

**Scottish
Parliament**

HOLYROOD ROAD

**Our Dynamic
Earth**

THE CANONGATE

The Canongate (the gait or road of the canons of Holyrood Abbey) was a separate burgh until Edinburgh council purchased it in 1636. It was developed late and less densely than the area within the city walls so it was here that the Court nobility built their large houses until the Union of the Crowns. It remain the fashionable area until the development of the New Town when it then became an industrial district. After World War Two much of the housing in this part of the city walls was restored or rebuilt; and recently, as industry has moved away, the larger sites have been redeveloped for example as the Scottish Parliament and the Our Dynamic Earth exhibition.

painted in a rather insipid cross between pink and maroon, is the **Tass** **2**. Despite this, and the curious name reminiscent of the unlamented old Soviet news agency, but which actually recalls a Scots drinking vessel, this is arguably the best destination on the Royal Mile for lovers of cask beer and traditional pubs. The welcoming interior, pleasantly unspoilt with plenty of dark wood, is quite small although there's a little formal dining room up some stairs at the rear. Deuchars IPA is accompanied by three rotating guest beers in good condition. Food, including MacSween's haggis, is served until late with

The Palace of Holyrood

main courses for a fiver on Wednesdays.

Opposite the Tass is the *World's End* pub – named because here stood the Netherbow Port, the imposing looking eastern entrance to the city. Tolls were charged on people entering; and the poor of Edinburgh could not afford to pay to re-enter so their world ended at the gates, within which they were in effect trapped. The spikes of the gate were used to impale the heads of executed criminals, presumably *pour décourager les autres*, rather like at London's

left: **The Tass** right: **The Tollbooth Tavern**

Temple Bar. Sadly there is no trace of the impressive building today but brass markers in the road trace the outline of the old gate perimeter.

Head down into the Canongate (see box) which is much quieter but has some interesting shops including Cadenheads whisky emporium and a Scottish historical map shop. The Canongate Tolbooth dominates the next stretch of the street – an impressive late 16th century building, it towers over the footway and a huge clock projects out overhead. As the name implies it was used to collect fees from people entering the burgh; it has had a variety of functions since including prison and council chamber. Today part of it houses the

Sanctuary buildings, Abbey Strand

People's Story, a museum telling the story of ordinary folks' lives in the city – and part contains the **Tollbooth Tavern** 3. A pub since about 1820, it's long and narrow with a carved bar front and small but attractive gantry. An upper room at the back, formerly a separate house and now used as an eating area (food is served daily) was absorbed into the pub later. There are views out to Calton Hill. The ales are the two popular 'usual suspects' from Caledonian Brewery.

A few yards downhill is the Canongate Kirk (1688). Its attractive frontage has a touch of Dutch influence, maybe because it was completed under James's successor, William of Orange. It was built to replace Holyrood Abbey, which had hitherto served as the parish church of the Canongate. The kirkyard is well worth a visit, both for the views across to Calton Hill and the interesting collection of monuments including one to Adam Smith, the adopted guru of the free market evangelists.

Just past Canongate Kirk take a short detour down Dunbar's Close on your left, which brings you out into Dunbar's Close Garden, an unexpected oasis of tranquillity now run by Edinburgh City Council. The gardens are laid out in the manner of a 17th century garden and, unlike most of the Royal Mile, you'll often have the place to yourself, so take some time to explore and appreciate it.

Just before the foot of the Royal Mile on the left is the picturesque White Horse Close, worth a peek, but by now the view is dominated by the

Palace of Holyrood and its brash new neighbours. This guide cannot do justice to Holyrood, but adjacent to the splendid house are the ruins of Holyrood Abbey, built in 1128 by order of King David I. It was converted to a Roman Catholic chapel in 1688 by James II and then plundered after the Glorious Revolution. It was partially restored but finally finished off in a gale in 1768 which took the roof away...

The attractive baroque palace of course, official residence of HRH when north of the border, is most closely associated with Mary, Queen of Scots. If you like your history you'll want to spend time in here. The relatively humble

> ### EDINBURGH'S CLOSES
>
> For a more complete companion to the numerous closes and wynds that link the Royal Mile with the lower areas north and south, try *Walks in Edinburgh's Old Town* by Michael and Elspeth Wills or see www.edinburgh-royalmile.com/closes/royalmile-closes.html. If you're energetic it's well worth nosing into some of them, in addition to those on the route.

buildings in Abbey Strand at the entrance to the palace are in an attractive vernacular style in contrast to the formality beyond the gates. Running across the road junction at Abbey

John Knox House

left: **The Regent** right: **The Regent interior**

Strand are a number of 'S' shapes. These mark the boundary of the religious sanctuary provided from civil law by Holyrood Abbey. Facing Holyrood Palace stands the extravagant new Scottish Parliament complex which opened for business on 7th September 2004. The design vision of the development came from the late Catalan architect, Enric Miralles, who died in the early stages of construction. The closely grouped parliament buildings have a supposedly nautical theme, with the towers being built in the shape of boats with upturned keels as their roofs! The project was mired in a great deal of controversy, partly due to the ever escalating costs (nothing new there for public buildings) but the striking design so close to the palace opposite upset many traditionalists. Others have a more positive view of the place; you can make your own mind up; but you can go into the viewing gallery of the debating chamber inside, which has found wide favour.

The futuristic looking tent behind is Dynamic Earth, mainly aimed at schoolchildren and Scotland's answer to the Natural History Museum.

On a sunny day the open spaces leading directly from the Palace grounds and running up to the volcanic sill of Salisbury Crag make a good place for a siesta; but to reach our final pub bear left onto Abbeyhill, and it's a five minute walk along the road, under the railway bridge, and up to the junction at the top. If you can't face the walk, the 35 bus will carry you up. Right on the corner here is the **Regent 4**. In the midst of the city's 'pink triangle' this attractive tenement bar bills itself as 'Edinburgh's gay pub' but offers a welcome to all. The interesting layout features a horseshoe bar and two partially opened out rooms with a variety of seating from decadent leather sofas and armchairs to a gymnastic pommel horse on the way to the facilities! Alongside Deuchars IPA there are two changing guest beers, with something from Harviestoun often available and Old Rosie's cider on the other handpump. The Regent won the Edinburgh and Lothian CAMRA branch Pub of the Year award in 2010, no mean feat in a city with so many good bars to choose from.

> LINK

PUB INFORMATION

1 The Mitre
131-133 High St, Edinburgh EH1 1SG
0131 652 3902
www.classicpubs.co.uk/
themitrebarroyalmileedinburgh
Opening Hours: 10 (12.30 Sun)-
11 (midnight Thu-Sat)

2 Tass
167 Canongate, Edinburgh, EH8 8BN
0131 556 5348
Opening Hours: 11 (12.30 Sun)-
11 (midnight Fri & Sat)

3 Tolbooth Tavern
1 High St, Edinburgh, EH1 1SR
0131 556 6338
Opening Hours: 11 (12.30 Sun)-
midnight (1am Thu-Sat)

4 Regent
2 Montrose Ter, Edinburgh, EH7 5DL
0131 661 8198
Opening Hours: 11 (12.30
Sun)-1am

> LINK Walk 3 **Over Calton Hill to Broughton** (page 29). Follow Regent Road west into the city centre to pick up the start of the Calton Hill route.

Rose Street and the Early New Town

Start/Finish: Waverley Steps

Access: Trains to Waverley, buses to Waverley Bridge and Princes Street

Distance: 1.6 miles (2.6km)

Key attractions: Scottish National Portrait Gallery, St. Andrew and St. George church, the Dome, Assembly Rooms, Georgian House (National Trust), West Register House

The pubs: Kenilworth, Oxford Bar, Abbotsford Bar

Links: to walks 1 and 7

A fairly short but very rewarding stroll around the grid-iron streets of Craig's New Town turns up some of the city's best pub interiors, each of which offers a good range of ales, plenty to see, and taken together, no shortage of eating possibilities. Like so much in this city it's a route of contrasts: pedestrianised Rose Street has become one of Edinburgh's tourist drags with its array of tartan-oriented shops, but even here there are some gems to be found. And the surrounding fine avenues and squares are a match for anything Europe has to offer in terms of urban architecture, with plenty of cultural destinations if you want to space out your drinking and make a day of it.

The Aitken founts at the Abbotsford dispense a changing range of excellent ales from Scottish microbreweries

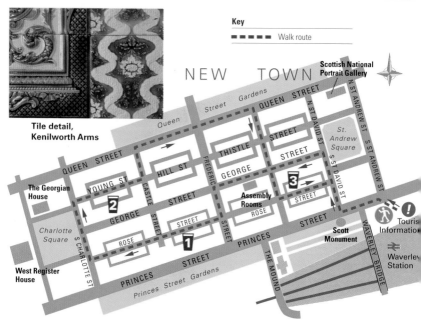

Tile detail, Kenilworth Arms

NEW TOWN

Key

■ ■ ■ ■ ■ Walk route

Scottish National Portrait Gallery

The Georgian House

Charlotte Square

West Register House

Assembly Rooms

Scott Monument

Tourist Information

Waverley Bridge

Waverley Station

St. Andrew Square

Follow the instructions for walk 1 as far as St. Andrew Square, but instead of turning right along the south of the square, cross South St. David Street and turn left into George Street, the next entry beyond Rose Street. A cultural diversion which may be of interest is the Scottish National Portrait Gallery on Queen Street. To get there, continue on North St. David Street to the junction and turn right (2-3 mins). It's worthwhile for the historical associations as well as its artistic merit, and was the world's first purpose-built portrait gallery (1889), but is closed until late 2011 for a major refurbishment.

George Street was conceived as the main axis of Craig's planned New Town, and if one could remove the traffic and street furniture it's still an impressive and imposing avenue with relatively few casualties architecturally. It quickly became Edinburgh's financial district, and although this has now moved to Lothian Road, compared to Princes Street it remains firmly upmarket. The handsome church of St. Andrew and St. George a short way down on the right dates from 1784 and was the first place of worship in the New Town. Inside, the Adam-style ceiling is a must see if you enjoy that sort of thing. In 1843 it was from here that

left: **Mosaic floor at the Dome**   right: **The splendid ceiling of the Dome**

nearly 500 ministers marched to Canonmills to establish the Free Church of Scotland. Opposite is the impressive *Dome*, once a bank with a truly sumptuous interior and worth sneaking in just to take a look at the fittings or even for a drink! (For description see route 25.) Further down on the left the Assembly Rooms date from 1787, and are the venue for CAMRA's Scottish Real Ale Festival in June.

Cross Hanover Street, noting the excellent view northwards (right) across Stockbridge towards the Firth of Forth and Fife, and continue as far as the junction with Frederick Street. Here turn left and take the first right into the pedestrianised Rose Street. This narrow lane between George and Princes Streets has become one of the main tourist axes of the city and is lined with a range of shops, restaurants and bars. Among the best of these is our first stop, the **Kenilworth** 7 at No. 152.

The Kenilworth is one of Edinburgh's impressive island bar pubs. The walls are covered in blue and white Minton tiles and above them is a patterned plasterwork ceiling. The pub was built in the late 18th century and despite a costly make over in 1966 much of the late Victorian interior survives including the bar counter which is a very solid

mahogany affair. Note the stained and leaded glass windows on the front and side of the first floor area. At the rear of the pub is a small room which is a good place to eat, and food is served all day. There's a good selection of real ales between the almost mandatory Caledonian brace, and three guests. You may even be able to inspect the current offerings simply by looking through the large front windows. In good weather outside seating offers an opportunity to sit and watch the tourists milling up and down…

Moving on, continue along Rose Street crossing Castle Street. The inspiration for the name is obvious if you glance left! Rose Street ends at

South Charlotte Street where turning right brings you immediately to the south eastern corner of Charlotte Square. Designed by Robert Adam this is one of the most attractive open spaces in the city centre. In perfect symmetry with St. Andrew Square at the other end of George Street it was originally (in Craig's plan) named St. George's Square but later re-christened in honor of George's Queen and/or third daughter, Charlotte. In the centre is an equestrian statue of Albert the Prince Consort. The northern side of the Square is particularly impressive thanks to Adam's palatial facades. No. 7 is the National Trust for Scotland's Georgian House offering a great insight into the lives of the upper classes

Ceiling detail at the Abbotsford

of the 18th century, and should ideally be visited in conjunction with Gladstone's Land (see walk 4) on the Royal Mile. Incidentally, culture vultures may also be interested in the West Register House, with its green dome. Here are housed some of Scotland's greatest historical documents, not least the declaration of Arbroath (1320), Robert the Bruce's defiant declaration of Scottish independence. For literature fans, Charlotte Square Gardens is the home of the Edinburgh International Book Festival during the last two weeks of August. LINK 1

Re-crossing George Street and reaching the northeastern corner of the square the next turning right is Young Street, which from looking on a

THE NEW TOWN

The pressure to create a New Town for Edinburgh came to a head in the middle of the 18th century, as conditions in the crowded old town continued to worsen and Edinburgh's bourgeoisie dearly wished to escape the squalor. The competition to submit a design was won by young architect James Craig around 1766 when he was still in his twenties. His scheme consisted of three parallel main streets, with George Street, (named after the reigning monarch, George III) being the widest and grandest main thoroughfare, and Queen Street and Princes Street (in honour of George's two sons) running to the North and South respectively. Two narrower lanes or 'meuse' (mews) serviced them: Rose Street, and Thistle Street (after the emblems of the two main states in the Union). Completing the grid are three north-south streets: Castle, Frederick

and Hanover Streets are named for the views of the castle, the father of King George and the Royal family name respectively. All very patriotic and suitably subservient!

Crossing points were built to access the new land; the North Bridge in 1772, and the Mound, which doubled as a tip for material excavated during construction of the New Town. As the successive stages of the New Town were developed, the rich moved northwards from cramped tenements in narrow closes into grand Georgian homes on wide roads.

Later phases of the New Town were built, notably north towards Stockbridge, and west into the Moray estate (see walks 7 and 9). Today, the New Town is by far the largest area of Georgian architecture in Europe.

The superb northern side of Charlotte Square

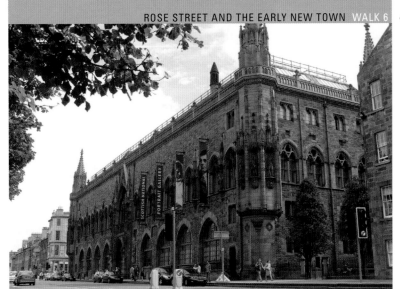

Scottish National Portrait Gallery

map is in perfect symmetry with Rose Street. In character however, it could hardly be more different. You might want to pop in at the *Cambridge Bar* at No. 20, particularly if you're calling in for one of its famous burgers, in which case you can wash it down with a pint of Deuchars IPA or a guest beer; but either way, a little further along on the right is the wonderfully unpretentious **Oxford Bar** ②. Undoubtedly the most unaltered bar in the city, this early 19th century drinking shop is a real gem and should be treated with the reverence that its gravitas deserves. It retains its opaque windows, something I think we need a campaign to restore in many other pubs; they still carry an advert for Bernard's India Pale Ale. Inside, the tiny 'main' bar is a stand-up affair with room only for a few stools and a window bench, but it oozes character. Up the steps and right is a larger but pleasingly spartan sitting room where like at the bar, conversation is the order of the day. It's worth a visit just to see the photo of the stern erstwhile guv'nor, Willie Ross, about whom all sorts of legends abound, probably most of them exaggerated. However, he certainly doesn't look like the sort of landlord to get on the wrong side of…

Let's not forget the beer: Belhaven Best, Deuchars IPA and two guests, often the excel-

lent Cairngorm Trade Winds. I suppose one ought to mention that many characters from Ian Rankin's Rebus novels use the pub; but happily, so far at least, the place hasn't been overrun by coachloads of trippers as a result – or for that matter, by weekend hen parties. Long may that continue.

Continue to the junction with Castle Street and turn left down to busy Queen Street – alternatively, a short detour to the right will take you to Sir Walter Scott's home at No. 39.

The gardens adjoining Queen Street were a concession to landowners who wanted a buffer zone between the first and second phases of the New Town development. Turn right and walk

The frontage of the Abbotsford Bar

left: **Caledonian pumpclips in the Kenilworth** right: **The bar gantry at the Abbotsford**

along, crossing the junction of Frederick Street where once again you can see the land falling away downhill quickly to the north. Take the next right, Hanover Street and walk up to and across George Street past the statue of George IV, to re-join the eastern section of Rose Street by turning left at the pedestrian precinct. A little distance along here is our final pub on the walk, the **Abbotsford Bar 3**, in red sandstone. Even after the previous two pubs this is one of Edinburgh's very best interiors with a place in CAMRA's National Inventory of historic pub interiors. It was designed by one of Edinburgh's most prolific pub architects, Peter Henderson, possibly for the owner Charles Jenner to serve as his work-men's eating and drinking hole – his famous department store is directly opposite. It has an exceptional Edwardian mahogany island bar with a sturdy gantry, and, in the cor-ner, a separate snack counter. Your eyes will also be drawn upwards to the ceiling where there is some tremendous plasterwork. To complement this you can enjoy a range

of reliable real ales dispensed from one of the best surviving sets of traditional Scottish Aitken fonts. The beer range is continually changing but has a focus on Scottish micro-breweries. If you're finishing here and looking for food you are in luck as the upstairs restaurant opens lunchtimes and evenings.

From the Abbotsford, it's a short step back to Princes Street. Walk up the final few yards of Rose Street and turn right to rejoin South David Street at the corner of St. Andrew Square. ▶**LINK 2**◀

PUB INFORMATION

1 Kenilworth
152/154 Rose St, Edinburgh, EH2 3JD
0131 226 1773
Opening Hours: 10-1am
CAMRA National Inventory (Part 2)

2 Oxford Bar
8 Young St, Edinburgh, EH2 4JB
0131 539 7119
www.oxfordbar.com
Opening Hours: 11-midnight (1am Thu-Sat); 12.30-11 Sun
CAMRA National Inventory (Part 1)

3 Abbotsford Bar
3/5 Rose St, Edinburgh, EH2 2PR
0131 225 5276
www.theabbotsford.com
Opening Hours: 11-midnight; 12-11.30 Sun
CAMRA National Inventory (Part 1)

▶**LINK 1**◀ Walk 7 **Squares and Crescents of the New Town** (page 51) For a longer trail, pick up walk 7 at Charlotte Square; or better still, return there after the Oxford Bar!

▶**LINK 2**◀ Walk 1 **Waverley Circuit** (page 19) From the Abbotsford, walk into St. David Street to join the start of walk 1.

Squares and Crescents of the New Town

WALK INFORMATION

Start: Charlotte Square

Finish: St. Andrew Square

Access: Buses 19 and 36 from Princes Steet, 41 from George IV Bridge, and 37/47 from Nicholson Street and the Bridges

Distance: 1.75 miles (2.8km)

Key attractions: Charlotte Square, National Trust Georgian House, Moray Place terraces

The pubs: Kay's Bar, Clark's Bar, Cumberland Bar, Star Bar

Links: to walks 3, 6 and 9

This walk is a celebration in stone from start to finish, right down to the setts which have survived in nearly all the streets here. The early New Town has largely been colonised by commerce, but further north the early 19th century developments make up the largest unspoiled area of Georgian houses – mainly in the form of grand residential terraces and circuses (circular crescents) – that you'll find anywhere. The route here takes in some of the very best architectural sights in the New Town. At first glance the area gives the impression of being pub-free – however, hidden away from the gaze and patronage of the casual tripper and the troupes of hen-and-stag parties milling around the city centre at weekends are some nice little gems to revitalise you as you go about your sightseeing.

Start at Charlotte Square – only a short step from the west end of Princes Street, but if you're coming from Waverley and points south the buses you want are 19, 36, 41 (from George IV Bridge), and 37/47 (from Nicolson Street and the Bridges).

When Robert Burns referred to 'heavenly Hanoverianism' he probably had Charlotte Square in mind. Robert Adam was commissioned to come up with a unified scheme for the whole square, and although he died with only the superb northern side complete, the rest is

The stunning terraces of Moray Place

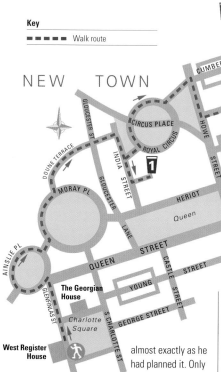

Key

▪ ▪ ▪ ▪ ▪ Walk route

NEW TOWN

almost exactly as he had planned it. Only Robert Reid's domed church on the west side, now West Register House (see walk 6), was an addition, and not a bad one at that. From an architectural perspective the Square is undoubtedly one of Europe's finest achievements. It's a pity, as it often is, that the intrusion of traffic is significant; and that access to the central garden is strictly *verboten*. On the northern side, the National Trust for Scotland have restored No. 7 as the 'Georgian House' intended to reflect living conditions for the affluent at the time (the NTS 'Gladstone's Land' property in the Lawnmarket, walk 4, offers a lower class contrast). ▶LINK 1◀

Head round to the western side (by West Register House) and walk northwards (with the traffic) briefly leaving the vehicles behind by continuing straight ahead into Glenfinlas Street.

This leads you downhill to a junction where heading left quickly brings you into the Georgian circus of Ainslie Place. This is part of the Moray Estate built by James Graham from 1820 onwards, and like much of the classical New Town it has survived relatively intact. Turning left and

walking round to the far side of the circus leads you away from the traffic as the near side is now a through route into the city. Ainslie Place leads north east out into Moray Place, which is the grandest of all Edinburgh's Georgian circuses. The sheer elegance and scale of the buildings is quite breathtaking and you'd need a lot of money to buy an address here. The green in the middle, like most of the open spaces in the New Town, was created as a private retreat for the wealthy residents, and that's what it remains. Walking clockwise around the terrace, take the first turning to the left, which leads down and around the corner into Doune Terrace, with good views across the rooftops of Stockbridge. The fantastic gothic fantasy-cum-chateau you can see piercing the skyline beyond is Fettes College, one of Scotland's top independent schools. Cross narrow Gloucester Lane before turning right at the T junction into India Street. You are now facing the gardens of the Royal Circus, but we will return this way shortly so for now continue uphill on India Street and take the second turn left into Jamaica Street West. On the next corner is our first port of call, **Kay's Bar** 1 . This former wine merchants has only been a pub for some 35 years, but in keeping with its surroundings it's one of the classiest in the city, so it might be as well to silence mobiles with tacky ringtones and be on your best behaviour! With its handsome stonework and gable end shopfront appearance, it's a very attractive building; and this goes for the inside too where the small main bar room offers into another room lined with books. Alongside national brands from Caledonian and Theakston, you can expect some interesting guests among the array of handpumps on the bar, and the pub often makes it into the *Good Beer Guide*.

A favourite retreat of the well-heeled silks and other professionals living hereabouts, it can get very busy; and prices are high even by Edinburgh standards, although you may consider the 10% premium worth it to take your ale in such convivial surroundings. There's also, as you might expect, a serious range of single malt whiskies. Food is available at lunchtimes.

Return to India Street and return downhill, but only as far as the next turning right which leads directly to Circus Gardens, another of the New Town's favoured addresses. This one has a fairly busy road running through the middle though, so it's not as secluded as Moray Place. We're now in the district of Stockbridge which is one of the city's favourite addresses with its bohemian atmosphere and plenty of good things to look at (see walk 9). Head clockwise around the Circus and cross Circus Place, and passing another impressive terrace take the first exit left (North East Circus Place) which brings you almost immediately to a T junction where you turn

Clark's Bar has the most unspoilt interior on the walk

right, then first left into wide and spacious Great King Street. **LINK 2** Looking at the map you can see that Great King Street and its satellites Cumberland and Northumberland Street on either side mimic the layout of James Craig's original New Town where George Street is the central road. Walk down Great King Street as far as the first junction and turn left into Dundas Street. This is another wide avenue, named after Henry Dundas, a big noise in late 18th century Scottish politics. He was the Government's man in Scotland, distributing largesse to the nobility and generally batting for the rich. Just beyond the first crossroads on the left-hand side you'll see the simple name sign of **Clark's Bar** **2** close to the foot of the hill. This is a classic late Victorian tenement bar whose unspoiled interior still carries some gravitas from the period. Below the dark red ceiling, and the walls with their dado panels and old mirrors sit brass table tops and red leather benches. The real gems here though are the two cosy, panelled rear snugs, which were recently rumoured to be under threat but happily survive, so far at least. Use them or lose them! Beer range is limited to Caledonian Deuchars IPA and one, sometimes two guests, but for pub heritage devotees this is the highlight of the walk.

Classy Kay's Bar is a former wine merchants' shop

Leaving Clark's cross Dundas Street and retrace your steps as far as Cumberland Street. At the first junction, turn left and walk down to the far end of yet another handsome terrace of early 19th century Georgian architecture. At the far end is another well-hidden pub, the **Cumberland Bar** ▣. Another carefully refurbished pub from the people who brought you the *Bow Bar* (walk 2) and *Thompson's Bar* (walk 11), this popular New Town alehouse has eight handpumps, dispensing mainly Scottish microbrewery offerings, although Timothy Taylor Landlord is a regular here too. The interior has been designed to recreate the intimacy offered by the Victorian pub, with several partially opened out rooms and a wide variety of seating and standing areas. Meals are served throughout the day. The attractive sunken garden is a very popular draw especially in summer, the more so since few city pubs can offer one.

Coming out of the Cumberland turn right and right again into Dundonald Street which climbs steadily past the gardens of Drummond Place on your left. ▶LINK 3◀ At the top where the road bends round to the right into Northumberland Street a small mews leads off to the left and a few yards along, tucked nicely out of sight of the hordes of tourists who never get this far in any case, is the last pub of the walk, the **Star Bar** ▣. The pretty severe lines of the exterior give way to a cosy and welcoming split level internal layout with a small bar serving Deuchars IPA and Timothy Taylor Landlord. Lunchtime food is available until 2.30pm. Despite the premium on space they find room for a table football machine in one corner of the lower room. There's a minuscule

Eight beers and a garden await you at the Cumberland

outdoor terrace at the back but it can't compete with the Cumberland's garden and you're probably better off inside.

That completes the drinking; and if you want to get back to the city centre with the minimum of legwork, simply walk left out of the pub and along Northumberland Street until you return to Dundas Street, and take buses 13, 23 or 27 uphill. To return to the centre on foot, turn right out of the Star Bar through Dublin Meuse [sic] and right into handsome Dublin Street, and keep going, across Queen Street to reach St. Andrew Square. This provides a satisfying symmetry with the start of the walk but the Square is nowhere near as handsome as its counterpart.

▶LINK 1◀ Walk 6 **Rose Street and the Early New Town** *(page 45)* To visit the celebrated *Oxford* and *Cambridge Bars*, take Young Street at the north-east corner of Charlotte Square.

▶LINK 2◀ Walk 9 **Down to Stockbridge** *(page 59)* Simply bear left rather than right on exit from Northeast Circus Place and *St. Vincent's Bar* is just a few yards down the hill on the left.

▶LINK 3◀ Walk 3 **Over Calton Hill to Broughton** *(page 29)* Turn left into Drummond Place and exit into London Street at the far end of the gardens. At the end of this road the *Cask & Barrel* stands prominently on the opposite corner.

PUB INFORMATION

1 Kay's Bar
39 Jamaica St, Edinburgh, EH3 6HF
0131 225 1858
Opening Hours: 11-midnight
(1am Fri & Sat); 12.30 - 11 Sun

2 Clark's Bar
142 Dundas St, Edinburgh, EH3 5DQ
0131 556 1067
Opening Hours: 11 (12.30 Sun)-
11 (11.30 Thu-Sat)
CAMRA Regional Inventory

3 Cumberland Bar
1-3 Cumberland St, Edinburgh,
EH3 6RT
0131 558 3134
www.cumberlandbar.co.uk
Opening Hours: 10am-1am

4 Star Bar
1 Northumberland Pl, Edinburgh,
EH3 6LQ
0131 539 8070
www.starbar.co.uk
Opening Hours: 12-1am

Via the Meadows to Tollcross

WALK INFORMATION

Start: Waverley Steps

Finish: Tollcross

Access: Trains to Waverley, buses to Waverley Bridge and Princes Street

Distance: 1.5 miles (2.5 km)

Key attractions: National Museum and Royal Museum of Scotland, Greyfriars Bobby statue, the Meadows

The pubs: Sandy Bell's Bar, The Doctors, Bennett's Bar, Cloisters Bar

Link: to walk 2 and 13

On the south side of the Old Town the land falls away quite steeply just as it does to the north, and this presented another obstacle to the early development of Edinburgh. But beyond the Old Town's notorious Grassmarket with its public executions and the slums of the Cowgate, Edinburgh's first fashionable streets and suburbs developed, and our walk visits some of these. For reasons that will become clear the only fitting way of approaching this area, appreciating it in its historical context, is by the long viaduct of North Bridge and South Bridge; fortunately refreshments are at hand just when they're needed…

From Waverley Steps turn right along Princes Street, past the Balmoral Hotel, to reach the traffic lights, with the imposing Register House opposite (see walk 1). Turn right here and walk across North Bridge with fine views especially across to Arthur's Seat and Calton Hill and the National Monument/Disgrace, depending on your point of view (see walk 3) to your left. In 1765 work started on a bridge to link the ridge on which Edinburgh's Old Town was built, across the Nor' Loch to the ridge beyond it. This huge public works project was ostensibly to improve access to the port of Leith but it also facilitated

Across the Meadows looking towards Arthur's Seat and Salisbury Crags

the success of the yet-to-be-built New Town, the competition for the design of which (see walk 5) was just under way. North Bridge was completed in 1772, but was rebuilt in the late 19th century to accommodate Waverley station. By the time you arrive at the crossroads with the High Street (the Royal Mile) by the Tron church you're back at ground level, so to speak.

Continue straight ahead into South Bridge, which from here doesn't look like a bridge at all but is in fact a long viaduct of nineteen arches! Once the North Bridge had been built, the logical next step was to continue the route southwards, linking with the new fashionable southern suburbs: Nicholson Street had been laid out in 1757,

left: **Handsome terraces fronting The Meadows** right: **Stained glass windows at Bennet's Bar**

for example, and the handsome George Square in 1766. Fittingly it was Robert Adam who designed the Register House (at this time nearing completion) who was involved in the early plans to construct a viaduct over the valley of the Cowgate and although his flamboyant design was rejected, construction on South Bridge started in 1785. Today the only arch visible is the one across the Cowgate itself: tenement buildings were run up on either side obscuring the others. It was a very important episode in the expansion of the city, in which north-south communications remain difficult to this day. If you want to get an impression of the slope of the land either side of South Bridge then just have a look at Blair Steet, running down from Hunter Square which is on your right immediately beyond the Tron Kirk. The construction of buildings either side of the bridge arches also

helped to offset the high (almost £30,000!) cost of building the South Bridge. While you're here, if you fancy an early drink, **The Advocate 5** at No. 7 Hunter Square offers three real ales and is worth a punt. In about 200 yards the South Bridge crosses the Cowgate and you can look down on to this once important thoroughfare.

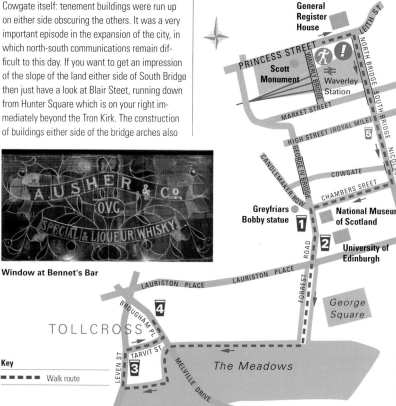

Window at Bennet's Bar

Key

▬ ▬ ▬ ▬ Walk route

After a further 150 yards turn right into Chambers Street. This imposing avenue was laid out shortly after the Lord Provost, William Chambers brought in his Edinburgh Improvement Act in 1867 an early attempt at bringing better town planning to the city. His statue can be found in the middle of the street. As you walk down look out for the Old College buildings of Edinburgh University on your left, completed around 1827, and at the far end the two complementary museums, the Victorian Royal Museum and the much newer (1998) Museum of Scotland. Together they make up a tremendous collection over several stories which is highly recommended, particularly if it's still before opening time! There's also a rooftop viewing gallery which offers great views over the city.

Across the street at the junction here is one of Edinburgh's major tourist attractions, which even has a pub named after it. If you arrive before the Japanese tourists you can read about Greyfriars Bobby for yourself by crossing the road to the small statue of the scruffy terrier sitting on a plinth at the junction with Candlemaker Row. Turn left or southwards here and keep right into Forest Road for just along here beyond the entrance to Grey Friars church, is our first refreshment stop, **Sandy Bells 1**.

Sandy Bells is a tiny corner pub named after the erstwhile proprietor who actually welcomed folk musicians into his pub when it wasn't fashionable so to do! It eventually took his name, and now boasts nightly folk music and also hosts afternoon sessions at the weekend. The characterful interior has changed little in the last half century and pub heritage fans will enjoy the old gantry and bar counter. At the rear is a small room; but seating is limited and there is always a lot of stand up drinking in the pub. Inveralmond Ossian is a frequent guest ale here alongside the ever-popular Caledonian Deuchars IPA and Courage Directors Bitter.

It's not far at all to the next stop – you won't have time to work up much of a thirst! From Sandy Bells continue south about a hundred yards to the junction and across the road is **Doctors 2**. This is a spacious 'L' shaped bar on a prominent corner site. Despite the open plan it manages to offer several distinct drinking areas, with half height screens around some of the seating, and plenty of opportunity for perpendicular drinking too. Being

Gantry at Bennet's Bar, Tollcross

very close to the University Quarter, it gets very busy in the evenings with a young crowd but with eight hand pumps offering two regular beers from Caledonian and up to six changing guest beers, this pub takes its cask ale seriously and is well worth a call. Meals are served all day.

Cross the road outside Doctors and take the wide pedestrian boulevard downhill past the new complex of recently converted student flats. **LINK 1** In a couple of minutes you'll reach The Meadows, the expansive open space at the heart of the south side. Like Princes Street Gardens this was once occupied by water, the Burgh or South Loch, and it was also a major source of the city's drinking water, as well as later playing host to both of the city's main football teams in their infancy. The sporting connection is retained on the adjacent Bruntsfield Links, which has the world's oldest short hole golf course, and best of all it's free! We are aiming for the eastern end of The Meadows, so pick a route – either bear right onto the foot and cycle path and follow the northern fringe of the open space, or if you prefer, stroll across The Meadows towards the busy road (Melville Drive) and the handsome Victorian villas and flats beyond it, bearing right all the while.

You'll eventually reach the point where the cycle path meets Melville Drive at a controlled crossing. Close by stand two commemorative pillars erected in 1886 in connection with the International Exhibition opened in that year by Prince Albert Victor. The shafts of the pillars are built up with stones cut with the names from the various quarries which have supplied Edinburgh with stone, although the pillars have now weathered to varying degrees. Once across the road make for the attractive sandstone terraces in the side street a few yards directly ahead of you and simply follow this street to the left as it curves around 90 degrees and runs down (with open parkland on your left and buildings on your right) to another main road in a short distance. Now simply turn right here and head down the 200 yards or so to reach the next pub, **Bennet's Bar 3**. Don't be put off by the stern sandstone façade with the opaque windows: it's a real gem, on account of its fabulous interior, second only to the *Café Royal* in the quality of its fittings. But before you go too far in, don't miss the stained glass windows advertising the long-defunct brewery which once occupied the adjacent site now home to the King's Theatre. Pause too, to look in at the tiny jug bar (left on entry) sadly neglected at the moment but a valuable survivor. The back gantry, tiled walls with dark wood and impressive mirrors, and the solid little tables all contribute to the charact… oh, I almost forgot, the beer… well, predictably, the two handpumps offer Caledonian Deuchars IPA and 80/-, but this is one to savour primarily for the architecture.

Coming out from Bennet's, turn right past the King's Theatre and right again into Tarvit Street then left into Drumdryan Street which curves round

to bring you very quickly out on Brougham Street, the continuation of Melville Drive. Almost opposite you'll spot what looks like a vicarage but is in fact **Cloisters 4**. Cloisters is indeed a former parsonage which has been skillfully converted into one of Edinburgh's best alehouses. The attractive stone frontage gives way to a convivial internal drinking space with bare floorboards and old church benches around solid tables. The handsome gantry boasts an impressive range of single malt whiskies. Its location gives it a good mix of clientele including a lot of students, many of whom can be seen sampling from the wide range of nine cask ales which the pub offers: some like Cairngorm Trade Winds and Timothy Taylor Landlord are regular fixtures; and there is always at least one beer from Edinburgh's Stewart brewery. But you can expect a continually changing range of interesting guests to satisfy the most discriminating of palates; and expect them to be on good form too. The place is frequently very busy but this should certainly not deter you from visiting; in addition food is available at lunchtimes and evenings. It's not a place to overdo it however as a visit to the toilet down the spiral staircase could become a rather precarious adventure…!

To get back to Princes Street and St. Andrew Square, it's best to head down to Tollcross junction (turn right, 2-3 minutes) and pick up buses 10, 11,15 or 16. In addition buses 23, 27 and 45 travel via the Mound and cross Princes Street into Hanover Street. **LINK 2**

PUB INFORMATION

1 Sandy Bell's
25 Forrest Rd, Edinburgh, EH1 2QH
0131 225 2751
Opening Hours: 11.30-1am;
12.30-11 Sun
CAMRA Regional Inventory

2 Doctors
32 Forrest Rd, Edinburgh, EH1 2QN
0131 225 1819
Opening Hours: 10-1am

3 Bennet's Bar
8 Leven St, Edinburgh, EH3 9LG
0131 229 5143
Opening Hours: 11-12.30am
(1am Thu-Sat); 12.30-11.30 Sun
CAMRA National Inventory (part 1)

4 Cloisters Bar
26 Brougham St, Edinburgh, EH3 9JH
0131 221 9997
Opening Hours: 12 (12.30 Sun)-
midnight (1am Fri & Sat)

TRY ALSO:

5 The Advocate
7 Hunter Sq, Edinburgh, EH1 1QW
0131 226 2749
Opening Hours: 10am-1am

LINK 1 Walk 13 **Into the Southside** *(page 75)* Cut through into George Square via the 40 yard path, opposite Sainsbury's halfway down this pedestrian avenue, to join walk 13 and head into the Southside via the *Dagda Bar*.

LINK 2 Walk 2 **Around the Castle** *(page 23)* Walk down to Tollcross and crossing busy Lauriston Place at the lights take the next right, the pedestrianised High Riggs, with views of the Castle ahead. At the top, take the second of the two roads to the left, Bread Street. You should be able to see the *Blue Blazer* about fifty yards down on the next corner.

Down the Water of Leith to Stockbridge

WALK INFORMATION

Start: Dean Village

Finish: Stockbridge

Access: Buses from Princes Street

Distance: 1 mile (1.6km)

Key attractions: Dean Village, Dean Gallery, Water of Leith Walkway, Stockbridge shops, Botanic Gardens (½ mile)

The pubs: Bailie Bar, St. Vincent's Bar, The Antiquary, Stockbridge Tap

Link: to walk 10

Although less than a mile from Princes Street, the atmosphere in bohemian Stockbridge feels a world apart from the tourists and the bustle of Edinburgh's city centre. The approach, along one of the most attractive stretches of the Water of Leith adds to the expectation. The weekend is a good time to do this walk, for then the interesting shops on St. Stephen Street are in full swing; and on Sundays The Antiquary's famous breakfast (see below) is on offer. Don't miss Raeburn Place with its specialist shops either. The pubs match the area — distinctive, characterful, and with plenty of choice; and you can relax after a few beers in Inverleith Park or the Botanic Gardens, both just a few minutes walk away.

From the city centre take a bus (19, 36, 37, 47 from Princes Street) to Randolph Crescent, the last stop before the bus goes over the Dean Bridge. It's only about 150 yards from the west end of Princes Street, so walking is an option if it's a fine day. Walk a little further down the road to the point where

Water of Leith at Dean Village

the main road curves to the right at the start of the bridge and you'll see two roads leading off to the left. The attractive house at the top here is Kirkbrae House which incorporates an inscribed panel from a granary which once stood below it on the river. The lower lane running down the hill is Bell's Brae. Walk down this promising looking lane and immediately you'll feel as if you're entering another world for it drops steeply down and deposits you at the foot of the brae by an old bridge over the Water of Leith. This

is Dean Village. At one time this was a thriving industrial community with around ten mills engaged in turning out bread for the growing city and nearby villages.

If you've time it's worth spending a few moments having a look around here… from the bridge the slender tower of Holy Trinity church perched precariously on the edge of the valley looks particularly impressive, whilst across the river, the collection of striking red sandstone buildings is Well Court, commissioned as model working class housing in the mid 1880s by philanthropist Sir John Findlay.

It's also possible to access the Dean Gallery, with its world-class collection of Dada and Surrealism and comfortable café, by climbing the hill on the opposite side of the river, but it's easier to get to from the footbridge further upstream (see walk 11).

When you're ready to continue take the good riverside path downstream (Miller Row: there's an information board about the site a few yards down on the left) and under the impressive Dean Bridge (more viaduct than bridge, in fact) built by Thomas Telford in 1832. A little further downstream on this attractive section of the Water of Leith Walkway lies St.

Bernard's Well. Legend has it that the well was originally discovered in about 1760 by some boys from Heriot's School. The waters were held in high regard for their medicinal virtues and the pump room that you can see today was commissioned in about 1790. It's occasionally open to the public (for information see Edinburgh council's website). Just beyond the well the valley opens out and you can see some of the attractive Georgian houses of Stockbridge. This area was laid out about 50 years later than the early New Town and much of it was developed by the painter Henry Raeburn (1756-1823) who owned two adjoining estates in the neighbourhood. The streets in front of you as you climb up to and cross the bridge ahead of you are particularly handsome. Once across the bridge turn sharp right and walk along Dean Terrace with the river on your immediate right, down into the centre of Stockbridge in just a couple of minutes.

Stockbridge (see box) is probably the most bohemian and sought-after of Edinburgh's neighbourhoods and still retains a good deal of its separate identity. You'll see from the map that our four pubs are

STOCKBRIDG

Map

- DEAN STREET
- DEANHAUGH STREET
- ST STEPHEN STREET
- LESLIE PL
- CARLTON ST
- DEAN TER
- KERR ST
- CIRCUS LANE
- HOWE STREET
- ROYAL CIRCUS
- CIRCUS PLACE
- ROYAL CIRCUS
- INDIA PLACE
- GLOUCESTER ST
- GLOUCESTER LANE
- INDIA STREET
- DOUNE TERRACE
- MORAY PLACE
- HERIOT ROW
- Queen Street Gardens
- MORAY PLACE
- QUEEN STREET
- AINSLIE PL
- N CHARLOTTE ST
- Water of Leith
- QUEENS FERRY RD
- BELLS BRAE
- BELFORD ROAD
- QUEENS FERRY RD
- RANDOLPH CR
- GREAT STUART ST
- BLENHEIM ST
- Charlotte Square

Key

■ ■ ■ ■ ■ Walk route

fairly close together, and of course you're at liberty to tackle them in any order! The route here will aim to finish at the Stockbridge Tap which is probably the destination that real ale aficionados will want to linger in; and it's also well placed for the interesting shops of Raeburn Place. So... cross to the other side of the road, turn right and at the traffic lights continue in the same direction to the next junction, St. Stephen Street, where on the corner down some steps is the basement

Dean Bridge over the Water of Leith Walkway

Bailie Bar 1. The attractive interior, a lot larger than it looks from the outside, is decked out in a classy style to match the neighborhood: red leatherette stools and benches sit on the carpet around a large island bar, with a real fire in one corner. There is a more formal dining area to the rear. On the bar there's a wide range of ales available to get the day's drinking off to a good start: Caledonian Deuchars IPA, Courage Directors Bitter and four rotating guests from Scottish micro-breweries. Food is available from 11-9 (5pm on Fridays), and you can even browse the newspapers whilst you drink.

Leaving the Bailie, continue up the hill passing (or indeed visiting) another branch of Mellis's excellent cheesemongers (see walk 2) on the way, and take the next turning left into Circus Lane. Here, you can see at first hand the gentrification of Stockbridge in the little mews workshops and cottages which today will fetch the Scottish equivalent of a King's ransom. The street curves around to your right and brings you out to a junction of several streets under the tall and rather severe lines of William Playfair's St. Stephen's Church. Here, immediately on your right and easy to miss were it not for the giveaway lantern on the

STOCKBRIDGE

After the creation of Edinburgh's Georgian New Town which began in 1767, building steadily progressed northwards to encompass the small villages along the river including Stockbridge and Dean Village. Stockbridge still has something of a village atmosphere about it, although it is only a ten to fifteen minute walk from Edinburgh city centre. Portrait artist Sir Henry Raeburn was an early resident, and he was responsible for much of its development. Stockbridge has a definite Bohemian vibe despite the onset of gentrification; it's been home to many actors and artists, musicians, poets and writers.

The original Mrs Doubtfire or "Madame Doubt-

fire" who inspired the novel of the same name by Anne Fine lived in Circus Place. These days the area is an expensive residential district, but the shopping street retains something of the 1950s with several staunchly independent retailers from an old fashioned barbers to Armstrong's fishmongers, Bowers the butchers and Herbie's deli; and if it's true that the quality of the charity shops says something about an area then Stockbridge has something – shopping guru Mary Portas is the latest to move into Raeburn Place with a new venture. Her manifesto is simple: to transform Britain's musty charity shops into trendy "destination" stores.

The pubs aren't bad either...

wall at the end of Circus Lane, is **St. Vincent's Bar 2**. This is an interesting and the cosy pub which manages to have plenty of atmosphere even when relatively empty. The dark woodwork gives it a very traditional feel, particularly in the fine bar back which incorporates a clock. Once again there is a good range of ales on offer: Caledonian Deuchars IPA and up to four rotating guests, with the Orkney brewery a favourite. This was the first pub in Edinburgh to offer third pint glasses, so you can try three different beers which arrive in a custom made wooden carrier. Food arrangements were undergoing change at the time of writing so if you want to eat here it's best to phone ahead and check. Moving off, walk across Circus Lane and into St. Stephen Street keeping the church on your immediate right. This road will lead you straight back into Stockbridge and the further end of it has a number of interesting and bohemian shops which come alive at the weekend. In absorbing the atmosphere it would be again quite easy to miss your next pub if you haven't got used to looking down by this time! For yes, **The Antiquary 3** is yet another basement bar, on the left-hand side of the street. It's a former bakery which has its own well and its own ghost. You can get an impression of the former usage in the cavernous shape of the ceiling in the far left corner. But it's a Tardis of a place with plenty of room to spread out around the large bar counter. As for the beer, again expect Deuchars IPA alongside two guest beers, usually Scottish and usually a light and a dark ale to choose from. Food service is sparse especially during the week, although there is lunch on Friday and Saturday until 4pm. However the big pull here is on Sundays

The Antiquary, a former bakery

when The Antiquary serves probably the most decadent pub breakfast in Edinburgh (11-3) from a huge menu, swiftly followed by Sunday lunch (1-6) washed down with the Sunday papers. So, no prizes for guessing which is the recommended day of the week to come to Stockbridge!

Assuming you can still move and have the stomach for more, continue to the end of St. Stephen Street and walk back downhill across the river into the centre of Stockbridge, this time continuing further down Deanhaugh Street to the junction with Raeburn Place on the corner. Here you'll find the **Stockbridge Tap 4**. Modernised in the light and airy contemporary style quite recently, the former Bert's Bar has been reborn as a specialist alehouse offering the widest and most interesting range of beers in the village. Cairngorm Trade Winds and Stewart 80/- are regulars alongside Caledonian Deuchars IPA, but on the other handpumps the chances are you'll come across something you haven't tried before or even heard of. There is a wide range of seating available in the L-shaped bar but at busy times many people prefer to stand. The food here is well regarded and at weekends is available throughout the day. **» LINK**

If you're heading back to the city centre the bus stop is almost outside, and frequent services on routes 24, 29 and 42 will all do the job.

LINK Walk 10 **The Botanic Gardens and Canonmills** (page 63). From the Stockbridge Tap you can seamlessly go straight into the start of the Botanic Gardens and Canonmills walk

---

PUB INFORMATION

1 Bailie Bar
2 St Stephen St, Edinburgh,
EH3 5AL
0131 225 4673
www.thebailiebar.co.uk
Opening Hours: 11 (12.30 Sun)-
midnight (1am Fri & Sat)

2 St. Vincent's Bar
11 St. Vincent St, Edinburgh,
EH3 6SW
0131 225 7447
Opening Hours: 11 (12.20 Sun)-
midnight (1am Fri & Sat)

3 The Antiquary
72-78 St. Stephen St, Edinburgh,
EH3 5AQ
0131 225 2858
www.theantiquarybar.co.uk
Opening Hours: 11.30 (12.30
Sun)-12.30am (11 Mon, 1am
Thu-Sat)

4 Stockbridge Tap
2-6 Raeburn Pl, Edinburgh, EH4 1HN
0131 343 3000
Opening Hours: 12 (12.30 Sun)-
midnight (1am Fri & Sat)

The Botanic Gardens and Canonmills

WALK INFORMATION

Start: Stockbridge

Finish: Canonmills

Access: From the city centre buses 24, 29, 42

Distance: 1.2 miles (2 km)

Key attractions: Botanic Gardens, Inverleith Park, The Stockbridge Colonies (Victorian model housing), Water of Leith Walkway

The pubs: The Orchard, McLachlan's Alehouse, Smithies Alehouse

Links: to walk 9

Edinburgh's Royal Botanic Gardens grew out of a 17th century Physic garden in the grounds of Holyrood House, with a couple of intermediate moves, finally relocating to its present Inverleith site in 1820. Covering over 70 acres of beautiful grounds around Inverleith House, the site is globally important for plant science and education as well as being a great place to visit. And unlike their London counterpart at Kew, admission to which would make a big dent in your beer kitty, entry to the Edinburgh garden is absolutely free! You have a choice of routes, with the option of taking in the Colonies alongside the water of Leith, and after you have finished your drinking in Canonmills, you can walk back to Stockbridge along the river if you still have any energy.

Botanic gardens

Orchard Bar, Canonmills

steps lead down to the river by the pizza restaurant. Follow the walkway down stream as far as the iron Falshaw Bridge in about 300 yards where steps lead up onto Glenogle Road. As the map shows, the Water of Leith Walkway doubles back a few yards to the left from here and then follows Arboretum Avenue which runs up alongside the river and then bears left uphill and thence on to the West Gate of the Royal Botanic Gardens. If you take this direct route you can rejoin the instructions further down the page! It's a very worthwhile alternative however, especially for architecture and social history devotees to visit the Stockbridge Colonies (see box) by turning right on Glenogle Road and walking down past the attractive rows of terraces which in their day set new standards for workers' housing and even today are regarded as very 'des res' on the open market. Across the street is the Victorian swimming pool which is being restored and due to re-open

From the city centre take buses 24, 29 or 42 down to Stockbridge alighting at Deanhaugh Street just across the river bridge at the foot of the hill. If you don't need any retail therapy in this attractively bohemian suburb (see walk 9) LINK make for the bridge (north side) where

---

Royal Botanic

Gardens

ARBORETUM PLACE

INVERLEITH ROW

INVERLEITH TERRACE

Water of Leith

COLONIES

Water of Leith

GLENOGLE ROAD

BRANDON TER

CANONMILLS

1

2

3

Water of Leith

ARBORETUM AV

HENDERSON ROW

HAMILTON PLACE

Water of Leith

Key

▬ ▬ ▬ ▬ Walk route

• • • • • • Detour

▬ ▬ ▬ ▬ Alternative walk route

in summer 2010. At the far end of Colonies walk down Bells Place (signed Water of Leith Walkway) and a footbridge takes you across the river onto the Walkway. Here turn left and walk back to join the main route on Arboretum Avenue. If you don't want to visit the gardens, or it's too late and they are closed, you can turn right over the footbridge and simply follow the Walkway along river re-crossing the stream in about 300 yards and emerging in the centre of Canonmills at a point where the Orchard (see below) is a short distance up on the left.

Back on Arboretum Avenue, Inverleith Park stretches away on your left towards the spiky roofline of Fettes College, whilst to your right the new John Hope Gateway into the Botanic Gardens opens at 10am. Broadly speaking the gardens are open until 7pm in summer but close earlier at other times of the year (see www.rgbe.org.uk for more details). Put simply the gardens here – extending to over 70 diverse acres – are among the world's finest and well worth a

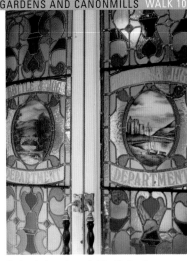

Stained glass doors in The Orchard

visit. When you emerge at the East gate onto Inverleith Row we're very close to our first pub stop which is a couple of hundred yards down on the right. **The Orchard** **1** is another

THE STOCKBRIDGE COLONIES

Right across Victorian Britain, reaction to the squalor of urban life for the working classes was growing and would lead to the birth of the Garden City movement at the end of the century. Scottish housing reformers sought an alternative to the traditional tenement which would enable a family to have their own garden and their own front door. There were several prototypes in Edinburgh and in 1861 the Edinburgh Co-operative Building Company was established. The site at Glenogle, on the south bank of the water of Leith, was quickly developed and by 1867 five terraces had been constructed.

A decade later the company had built over a thousand houses on this and four other sites in the city – perhaps the most notable success for co-operative housing ventures in Edinburgh's history. The Stockbridge Colonies, in two storey terraces, have a cottage style with high doors reached by outside stairs, but are also interesting in that the streets have an asymmetric structure – stairs on one side, street levels paths at the other, which make them quite unusual, especially in the midst of the Georgian New Town.

The Colonies

left: **Sunny afternoon at Smithies Alehouse** right: **McLachlan's Alehouse**

example of a traditional Edinburgh pub which has been given a very contemporary makeover, with a few traditional survivals hanging on amongst the modernity. The outside appears to have been treated with the same paint job as the *Stockbridge Tap* (walk 9). Inside it's airy and bright with floorboards and lots of light colours contrasting with the handsome old back gantry which has survived from a previous incarnation. The three doorways suggest a formerly divided up interior, and the entrance on the street corner retains some excellent stained glass in the internal doors. Although there are five hand pulls you can usually only expect Caledonian Deuchars IPA and occasionally a guest beer. Food is served all day until about 8.30pm.

Emerging from the Orchard, continue down the road crossing the Water of Leith and follow the road as it bends around to the left and climbs a short hill to the traffic lights. Across the road on your left is the *Stags' Head*, a splendidly traditional looking tenement pub, which sadly sells no real ale, but across the road to your right on the opposite corner is **McLachlan's Alehouse** ② which does. An interesting wedge-shaped corner bar with floorboards, wainscoting to the walls and green banquette seating, it offers two rotating beers one of which is always

from Edinburgh's Stewart brewery. There's a good variety of food available during the day.

You don't have to go far for the final pub on our short walk: turn right out of McLachlan's and walk about 50 yards along Eyre Place to find **Smithies Alehouse** ③. In contrast to McLachlan's or the Stags Head, this is a modern pub both inside and out but there are three well-kept beers, Deuchars IPA and two rotating guests. Another nice touch here is the attractive range of hand-painted mirrors featuring various fauna and flora, although these have to compete with a plethora of TV screens, mercifully not always switched on.

If you wish to walk back to Stockbridge, where you could do worse than visit some of the hostelries there, simply take the first right out of Smithies, and walk straight down to rejoin the Water of Leith Walkway by the bridge, and head backwards. To return to the city centre your best bet is a No. 8 bus from the stop close to the Stag's Head on the main road heading uphill. This will take you up to St. Andrew Square, Waverley and North Bridge.

PUB INFORMATION

① **The Orchard**
1-2 Howard Pl,
Edinburgh, EH3 5JZ
0131 550 0850
orchardbar.co.uk
Opening Hours: 11 (12 Sun)-1am

② **McLachlan's Alehouse**
1 Canonmills,
Edinburgh, EH3 5HA
0131 558 7080
Opening Hours: 11 (12.30 Sun)-1am

③ **Smithies Alehouse**
115 49-51 Eyre Pl,
Edinburgh, EH3 5EY
0131 556 9805
Opening Hours: 11-midnight (1am Fri & Sat); 12.30-midnight Sun

LINK Walk 9 **Down the Water of Leith to Stockbridge** (page 59) Kerr Street, on the south side of the river will take you to the basement bars of Stockbridge.

Roseburn Circuit

A longer route which will take you well away from the tourists into some of less fashionable districts, where transport history enthusiasts will have plenty to look at with railway yards and bridges carrying routes old and new mixed in with two different waterways. Culture vultures are well catered for within two of the city's best art galleries a short step from the route. To cap it all a couple of classic tenement pubs and a new one, risen phoenix-like, on the site of the old Fountain Brewery. Be warned that of all the routes in the book the pubs on this one are most likely to be thronged on football (Hearts) and Murrayfield rugby match days. Finally, it's a route best done in daylight since some short sections are less well frequented by passing foot traffic or vehicles.

Start by Haymarket station – which by the time you read this will hopefully have reverted to some sort of normality after widespread and sustained disruption for the new tram infrastructure – and, making for the station forecourt, cross the road bearing left to

walk along Haymarket Terrace taking the third turning off right, Magdala Crescent. Standing proudly in its own grounds across the street is the impressive former Donaldson's College which from its foundation in 1851 served as a school for deaf and other disadvantaged children until

The Union Canal towpath is popular with cyclists and joggers

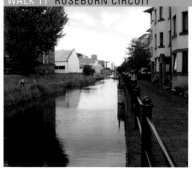

Union Canal at Fountainbridge

a new purpose-built Donaldson's was opened in Linlithgow in 2008. It's said that Queen Victoria complained jealously that this building, yet another in the enormous portfolio of William Playfair, eclipsed some of her own palaces! She may have had a point… it's a handsome building and the plans are to convert the interior into flats without compromising the stunning façade.

Walk to the far end of the Crescent passing some rather classy villas with their enormous bay windows. Right on the corner you'll find an inviting (or possibly daunting) stairway which drops down steeply into a wooded dell, at the bottom

of which lies the Water of Leith. It feels like you have entered a separate world from the bustle of Haymarket Terrace just five minutes ago. Turn left and follow the river upstream. The valley soon widens out at a bend by a weir, where a footbridge leads across and up to the Scottish Gallery of Modern Art and the Dean Gallery close by. If you need a cultural fix on this walk, this is the time to take it (see box).

With or without the arty *hors d'oeuvres*, follow the walkway under an old railway bridge (now a cycle path) and a short distance beyond, up a short flight of steps onto a quiet road which leads in 50 yards to the main road at Roseburn. Cross at the controlled crossing and walk back left to our first stop of the day, the **Roseburn Bar 1** on the next corner. At the foot of a four story Victorian tenement, this is a classic urban Scottish boozer. You'll enter first through a small former jug bar (off sales). It's then up a couple of steps into the huge public bar which really is the only place for the casual visitor to be if you're to soak in the character of the place; even though there's a separate lounge bar beyond. This bar must have one of the highest ceilings in Edinburgh, and beneath it, many of its old etched windows and brewery mirrors survive. Understandably, since both Murrayfield and Hearts' Tynecastle stadiums are little more than a stone's throw away the bar is largely dedicated to sport; but you can get a decent pint of Deuchars IPA which nestles among the founts of other fizzy products we don't talk about in polite company.

Leaving the Roseburn, head down Russell Street which runs at right angles away from the main road to the south. The huge maltings which once stood here is now gone and the area is a wee bit forlorn these days. There's a 90° bend to the left by the railway depot and

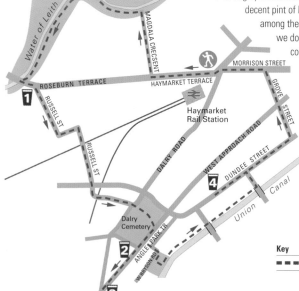

Scottish Gallery of Modern Art

Foot Bridge

Water of Leith

MAGDALA CRESCENT

MORRISON STREET

ROSEBURN TERRACE

HAYMARKET TERRACE

RUSSELL ST

Haymarket Rail Station

GROVE STREET

DALRY ROAD

WEST APPROACH ROAD

DUNDEE STREET

RUSSELL ST

1

4

Canal

Union Canal

Dalry Cemetery

ANGLE PARK TR

2

3

WEBRIDGE RD

Key

━ ━ ━ ━ ━ Walk route

then the cycleway you passed under earlier joins the road. Another 90° bend, and presently you bear left by two more bridges (one now carrying a road not a railway). You now rejoin 'civilisation' in the form of some traditional tenements, and keeping the green on your right walk to the main road in the district of Dalry. Right opposite is a small cemetery. Cross the road and bear slightly left to the gate – if it's open you can walk up through the cemetery to the top road (if you prefer to there's a footpath which runs up on the left hand side of the cemetery as you face it). Emerging onto what is Dundee Street, turn right and on the next corner you'll see the distinctive shape of your next pub at the foot of an apex of tenements. This the legendary **Athletic Arms** **2**, better known as the Diggers after two local cemeteries including the one you've just walked through.

Although locals will tell you it's a shadow of its former self, the place is still mightily impressive, like the Roseburn almost larger than life. It survived most of the 20th century with no major alterations although Scottish and Newcastle, who acquired the pub about 15 years ago have removed many of the screens and partitions that gave the pub much of its character. What does survive is a quaint little island gantry and a very good quality back gantry as well as a small back room. Red banquette seating runs along the walls flanked with dinky (and very practical) narrow tables, similar to those at the *Bow Bar*. This leaves a dance floor-sized area for perpendicular

drinking; and set into this floor, possibly to help disoriented sports fans find their way home after a heavy session' is an outsize compass rose. Although the place is certainly quieter now than in its heyday, you can still expect it to be packed when Hearts or the Scottish rugby team are playing at home. Celebrated for the legendary quality of its McEwans's 80/- for years, the pub now has an 80/- beer brewed by Stewarts, with Deuchars IPA and two guest beers mostly served from the traditional Aitken founts. Yes, the Diggers is still one of Edinburgh's classic pubs.

A short distance and further down Angle Park Terrace (the road on the right coming out of the Diggers) is a rather different type of bar, the **Caley Sample**

The bar at the Athletic Arms

The long bar at the Roseburn Tavern

Rooms 3. Compared to the Athletic Arms this is a very modern affair which doesn't quite do what it says on the tin – it's now owned by the same company who have the *Cambridge Bar* in Young Street (walk 6), and although you can sample Caledonian Deuchars IPA here as it's predictably their staple beer, there are usually two or three guest beers as well, and importantly for us this is perhaps your best bet on the walk to get a good slap-up meal from a wide-ranging menu. There's also an extensive wine list, probably part of an attempt (not alto-gether successful given the geography) to 'reposition the pub in the market place'.

Coming out of the Sample Rooms carefully cross the road and look for the footpath a short distance back on your left. It climbs some steps and at the top continues as West Bryson Road, still uphill, at 90° from the main road. The end of the street levels out and offers a view across a small park, beyond which runs the towpath

of the Union Canal, our next objective (see walk 20 for the history of the Canal). To get onto the path you need to head off to your right making for the prominent church tower, which will lead you to a gateway onto the canalside. Now we bear left and follow the canal almost to the end at Fountainbridge.

At the second overbridge, in about half a mile, take the sloping path just under the bridge up onto the street, and walk to your right downhill to join the main road. You're now back on Dundee Street which we visited earlier. Head back to your left and cross the road to the modern bay of big boxy shops set back from the street. This site was part of the large Fountain brewery originally built by William McEwan and surviving under Scottish & Newcastle until 2004, when the real ale part of the operation in the form of Caledonian was relocated to Slateford a mile or so further west. The better news is that at the far end of this retail complex stands **McCowans 4**. Probably the most unashamedly modern pub in the city, this two-level, bright spacious and airy emporium opened with its own brewhouse. This is currently mothballed, but the place offers Deuchars IPA and three guests, often from good Scottish micros. Seating is varied and comfortable, and there's plenty of space to stand around as well. There's a Wether-spoon-style menu if you need to eat, serving until 9pm daily.

You can get a bus back to city directly outside (buses 1 and 34 to Princes Street, or 35 will take you to Chambers Street and the Royal Mile). To return to Haymarket, retrace your steps back to Dundee Street and continue as far as the first turn left (a fair way down) which is Grove Street, and follow this to join Morrison Street close to *Thomson's Bar* just off to the right. **LINK**

PUB INFORMATION

1 Roseburn Bar
1 Roseburn Ter, Edinburgh, EH12 5NG
0131 337 1067
Opening Hours: 9am-11pm
(midnight Thu-Sat)
CAMRA Regional Inventory

2 Athletic Arms
1-3 Angle Park Ter, Edinburgh,
EH11 2JX
0131 337 3822
Opening Hours: 11 (12.30
Sun)-1am
CAMRA Regional Inventory

3 Caley Sample Rooms
58 Angle Park Ter, Edinburgh, EH11
0131 337 7204
www.thecaleysampleroom.co.uk
Opening Hours: 11.30-midnight;
10-1am Fri & Sat

4 McCowans
24 Dundee St, Edinburgh, EH11 1AJ
0131 228 8198
Opening Hours: 12-1am

LINK Walk 12
Edinburgh's West End (page 71) Pick up the start of the West End circuit from Haymarket.

Edinburgh's West End

WALK INFORMATION

Start/Finish: Haymarket rail station

Access: Trains and buses to Haymarket station from Princes Street

Distance: 1 mile (2.2 km)

Key attractions: St. Mary's Episcopal Cathedral, William Street shops

The pubs: Bert's Bar, Teuchters, Thomson's Bar, Ryrie's Bar

Links: to walk 11

A short circular walk around the well-heeled streets of the West End, which was developed steadily during the first half of the nineteenth century. In 1830 the Hay Market was at the rural-urban fringe of the city but the stately crescents to the north were laid out soon afterwards. The Cathedral of St. Mary's which dominates the first part of this walk, came later. In the mid 1840s the Caledonian Railway cut a linear swathe through the southern fringe of the West End to open their new Terminus on the Lothian Road in 1848 (see walk 2), but this is now occupied by one of the few significant areas of new buildings and roads in the city centre. The pubs will not disappoint, either in terms of beer range and quality, or architecturally.

Start at Haymarket station forecourt, as per walk 11 and cross the road outside the station. Bearing left take the first turning right which is Rosebery Crescent. Immediately you're confronted with another fine range of Edinburgh's trademark New Town terraces; these ones rather later than many, dating to the middle of the nineteenth century. At the top of the road swing

Ryrie's excellent wooden frontage still retains its original stained-glass windows

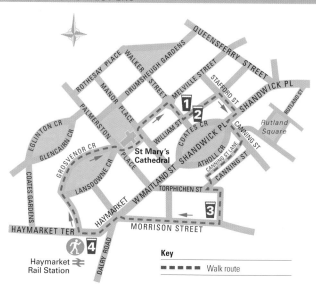

Key

▪ ▪ ▪ ▪ ▪ Walk route

around to the right into Grosvenor Crescent with its private central garden, and soon the towering spires of St. Mary's Episcopal Cathedral come into view over the treetops. Walk down to the end of the street and you are face to face with the largest church built in Scotland since the Reformation. Cross the road and walk through the cathedral grounds on the right hand side of the building which leads through to Manor place, admiring the scale and elegance of the cathedral. It was funded by a bequest from two wealthy unmarried sisters, Barbara and Mary Walker, to a design by Sir George Gilbert Scott (1811-1878), Britain's leading architect of the Gothic revival style who was also responsible for the Albert Memorial and St. Pancras Station in London. The central spire is 270ft high and aligned on an axis with Princes Street. The smaller two spires were added later during the First World War. It's arguably the most attractive church in the city and certainly the most dominant on the skyline. Cross Manor Place bearing slightly to your right to enter William Street which has now been rebranded as 'West End Village'. It's an attractive cobbled street which has been relatively tastefully gentrified with

St. Mary's Cathedral

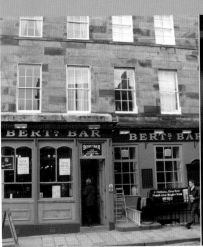

left: **Bert's Bar** right: **Teuchters interior**

a range of interesting and right on shops and would be worth a visit even if it did not contain a couple of decent pubs. Go straight ahead at the crossroads with statues to right and left (of Gladstone and Viscount Melville respectively) and you'll soon arrive at a pair of good real ale bars sitting literally opposite each other. **Bert's Bar** 1 is a traditional-style bar which has been taken firmly upmarket while retaining some of its character. There is a good back gantry and generally a lot of wood and tile work in evidence and a couple of a large brewery mirrors from Maclays of Alloa and Lorimer and Clark respectively. Best of all is the impressive range of nine hand pumps on the bar serving a changing range of interesting beers alongside Caledonian's 'anchor' favourites, 80 and Deuchars IPA. There's a wide menu serving food until 8pm (later during the festival) and the menu

Stained glass window at Ryrie's

is available on the pub website. Directly across the street is **Teuchters** 2 at the bottom of a handsome three story sandstone terrace. In many ways it has a similar formula to Bert's across the road – the wooden floorboards for example

– but it's in a more modern style with the trendy sofas making an appearance here. There are five hand pumps with Deuchars IPA, Timothy Taylor Landlord and rotating guest beers with Scottish maverick Brewdog seemingly popular at the moment. There's a huge whisky list and basic food although the eatery downstairs, the so-called 'Room in the West End' has a more extensive menu. Be warned that this must rate as one of the most expensive places in the city to drink cask ale so take plenty of money!

Continue down William Street to the next junction and turn right into Stafford Street and down to Shandwick Place the main road. Here, turn right having crossed the road and then take first left (by *Au Bar* which also offers real ale) into Canning Street. It's a pleasant little detour to take the first turning left into Rutland Square which despite its central location is a quiet little backwater and fairly unspoilt architecturally with handsome terraces around a central green with one or two mature trees. Back on Canning Street walk up and take the second turning on the right which is Canning Street Lane. This survives as

left: **Thomson's Bar** right: **Ryrie's Bar**

a quiet little mews although beyond this you're into the area which was formerly occupied by the railway lines of the old Caledonian Railway's Princes Street station (see walk 2) and has now been developed with brash modern buildings. At the far end walk up the hill and follow the traffic around on Dewar Place to join Morrison Street by the traffic lights at the top. Turn right here and a few yards down on your right is **Thomson's Bar 3**. Like the *Cumberland Bar* (walk 7) and the *Bow Bar* (walk 2) this attractive single room pub is one of the high-quality recreations of a traditional Scottish bar carried out by Ian Whyte all of which won him awards. In the case of Thomson's he salvaged much of the timber from yards (and a disused church) in Edinburgh and Glasgow. Interior carvings are based on designs of Alexander 'Greek' Thomson, a contemporary of Charles Rennie Mackintosh, and the excellent back gantry features mirrors inlaid with scenes from Greek mythology. The walls are adorned with mirrors from many long

defunct Scottish breweries. The good news applies to the beers too with no less than 8 tall founts dispensing a changing range of interesting ales. Lunches are served but no evening meals.

From Thomson's it's a very short walk down the hill back to Haymarket and as a reward for negotiating the busy junction the last stop of the day awaits you right next to the station. **Ryrie's Bar 4** is a great building inside and out. The excellent wooden frontage with a superb set of intact stained-glass windows is nicely complemented by the distinctive stepped gables. A smaller adjoining building on the right hand end of the pub houses a separate sitting room whose walls are lined with old photographs; but the main building is a long room fronting the bar counter. The decent back gantry is sadly partly obscured by a functional but hideous glass fronted case sitting above the bar counter, admittedly housing a good selection of whiskies. There are five cask beers: Caledonian 80 & Deuchars IPA; Greene King IPA & Speckled Hen; and Black Sheep Bitter. Meals are served all day. As with the pubs on walk 11 be warned that Ryrie's can get very busy indeed during football (Hearts) and rugby (Murrayfield) match days.

▶ LINK ◀

▶ LINK ◀ Walk 11 **Roseburn Circuit** (page 67) Pick up the start of the Roseburn Circuit from Haymarket.

PUB INFORMATION

1 Bert's Bar
1A Haymarket,
Edinburgh, EH12 5EY
0131 337 7582
www.bertsbar.co.uk
Opening Hours: 9am-1am

2 Teuchters
26 William St,
Edinburgh, EH3 7NH
0131 226 1036
www.aroomin.co.uk/teuchters
Opening Hours: 11am-1am

3 Thomson's Bar
182 Morrison St,
Edinburgh, EH3 8EB
0131 229 8684
Opening Hours: 12 (4 Sun)-
11.30 (midnight Thu & Sat;
1am Fri)

4 Ryrie's Bar
1A Haymarket, Edinburgh,
EH12 5EY
0131 337 7582
Opening Hours: 9am-1am
CAMRA Regional Inventory

Into the Southside

WALK INFORMATION

Start: Nicolson Square

Finish: Ratcliffe Terrace

Access: Buses from North Bridge to Nicolson Street

Distance: 1.5 miles (2.4km)

Key attractions: The Meadows, Southside shops, Leslie's Bar, Holyrood Park (0.25 miles)

The pubs: Dagda Bar, Abbey Alehouse, Old Bell, Leslie's Bar

Links: to walk 8

The Southside is a loose name for Edinburgh south of the Cowgate taking in the University buildings and extending across The Meadows into Marchmont and Grange. The young crowd here ensures that it's a vibrant part of the city with lively shops in Nicolson and Clerk Streets, including loads of charity shops if you like browsing, and plenty of cultural destinations (e.g. the Festival Theatre). The pubs are lively, and in Leslie's you'll see one of the best interiors in the city. This is a short walk, but you're never very far from Holyrood Park, and the more energetic can combine a visit here with an ascent of Salisbury Crags and/or Arthur's Seat — ideally *before* the drinking!

Abbey Alehouse

The Dagda Bar

To get to Nicolson Square by bus simply take any bus from the stops on the North Bridge. It's about half a mile; or you can walk, perhaps following the Tollcross route in walk 8 to The Meadows and turning left onto the footpath, omitting the first few hundred yards of the route

published here, but none of the pubs!

The square is a pleasant little oasis immediately on the right of Nicolson Street, and at the far end in the basement of the Nicolson Square Methodist church (1815) is the Square Centre Café, open from 8.30am. Move off south on Nicolson Street and, unless you're travelling on to do the charity shops, take the first turning right into West Nicolson Street where you'll find one two other pleasant eateries, including the renowned Mosque Kitchen, which aims its cheap and cheerful Indian style food mainly at students but is a good value and tasty standby if you don't mind eating from cardboard plates and you don't want to waste drinking time waiting for food to arrive.

Go straight over busy Potterow via the crossing and into Windmill Place, and you're suddenly in the university precinct. Just ahead in broadly the same direction (don't bear left with Windmill Place but straight ahead past the concrete slabs) lies George Square. At one time this was one of Edinburgh's most fashionable

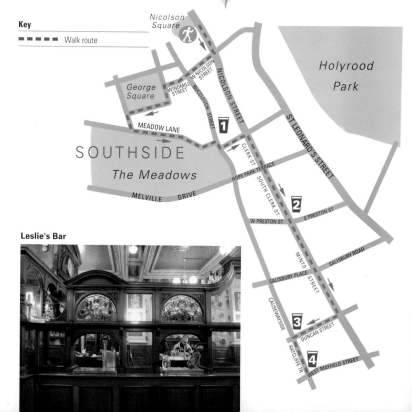

Key

▬ ▬ ▬ ▬ Walk route

Leslie's Bar

Nicolson Square

addresses; however today it has largely been annexed, and some might say ruined, by the University with a jumble of brutalist concrete and glass boxes, particularly along the east and south sides. Walk round the square to the west side where some pretty terraced houses survive, and head downhill where the lane brings you out onto The Meadows (for description see walk 8). Head eastwards (left) along the shared path past the tennis courts and take the second lane running up on the left near the end of the courts. This is called Boroughloch, and a short distance up this narrow cobbled street is the old entrance to the Boroughloch Brewery, once a successful and indeed pretty large business run by Melvin and Co. You and still see the sign above the archway although brewing ceased here over a century ago.

Boroughloch winds up to join Buc-cleuch Street and almost opposite is the first pub of the walk, the **Dagda Bar 1**. Since a makeover in about 2005 this externally unassuming Southside bar previously called Proc-tors has improved steadily. Inside it's small but has a welcoming, pubby atmosphere with homely banquette seats and some tables made from recycled casks, more suited for per-pendicular quaffing. It offers up to three well-kept changing cask ales mostly from Scottish micros, and a range of interesting continental beers too. Be warned however that on nights when a quiz is taking

place or if there's a group of noisy students in, there's nowhere to escape, but that said it's certainly one of my favourite Edinburgh bars.

Head left out of the Dagda and take the first left into Gifford Park with views of Salisbury Crags straight ahead. Turn right into South Clerk Street and across at the lights. Along on the left before the next lights is stop number two, the **Abbey Alehouse 2**. A festival alehouse with something of the corporate makeover inside, it's nonetheless an attractive interior with some sense of compartmentalisation remaining – guest beers are from the Punch Taverns list.

Continue on the main road south where there are some interesting shops to browse as you go – the road becomes Minto Street, and you'll notice the buildings becoming more spacious as you move into the well heeled southern suburbs. Look for Duncan Street on the right after another set of traffic lights, and walk down here to the end, where on the corner sits the **Old Bell 3**. A place of some antiq-uity, although

The Old Bell

Queen's Hall, Southside

the modern all-round external windows might suggest otherwise; the interior is better and retains something of an olde world feel with several secluded corners and dark leathery seats to complement the bar stools. The two beers are Caledonian Deuchars IPA as the regular and a changing guest. Food is available lunchtimes and evenings, and there's the sister establishment, the well-regarded New Bell restaurant upstairs to which you may want to return after finishing the pubs…

From the Old Bell it's a short and simple saunter to the last pub – and it's an Edinburgh classic to end this route. Walk south down the main road on the same side and you'll see the clock projecting over the pavement before you reach the sandstone tenement housing **Leslie's Bar** 4. A magnificent island-bar pub built in 1899 in by noted pub architect P. L. Henderson, it has one of the finest ceilings you'll see in an Edinburgh pub but the unique feature here is in the left hand saloon where an ornate wooden screen sits on the bar counter, punctuated by semi-circular serving apertures. This afforded privacy to customers of higher social standing. The mahogany central bar section complete with original Bryson clock remains almost entirely unaltered, and there are other delights here too for the architecture enthusiast (see walk 25). This is not a pub to get a sit down meal but they take their drinking seriously here. Not only is there a fabulous range of malt whiskies (and a detailed array of tasting notes on the pub's website), there's a wide range of constantly changing ales dispensed from up to six handpumps, so the taste buds will be as satisfied as the eyes when you're done. Definitely a bar of superlatives.

Buses 42 or 67 (opposite side of street) will take you back to the city via George IV Bridge. Or walk back to Minto Street for a wider range of buses.

▶ LINK ◀

PUB INFORMATION

1 Dagda Bar
93-95 Buccleuch St, Edinburgh,
EH8 9NG
0131 667 9773
Opening Hours: 12 (12.30 Sun)-1am

2 Abbey Alehouse
65 South Clerk St, Edinburgh,
EH8 9PP
0131 668 4862
www.abbeybar.co.uk
Opening Hours: 10am (10.30 Sun)-12.30am (1am Fri & Sat)

3 Old Bell
233-235 Causewayside,
Edinburgh, EH9 1PH
0131 668 1573
Opening Hours: 11-12 (1am Fri & Sat); 12.30-12 Sun

4 Leslie's Bar
45/47 Ratcliffe Ter, Edinburgh,
EH9 1SU
0131 667 7205
www.lesliesbar.com
Opening Hours: 11-11 (11.30 Thu; 12.30am Fri & Sat); 12.30-11.30 Sun
CAMRA National Inventory (Part 1)

Leslie's Bar

▶ LINK ◀ Walk 8 **Via the Meadows to Tollcross** (page 55) Take bus 42 or 67 from across the street and alight outside Sandy Bell's, Forrest Road, for walk 8.

Holyrood Park, Duddingston and the Innocent Railway Path

WALK INFORMATION

Start: Holyrood Palace

Finish: Duddingston or St. Leonard's Street

Access: Bus 36 from Waverley Bridge

Distance: 4.5 miles (7.2km)

Key attractions: Holyrood Palace; Scottish Parliament; Our Dynamic Earth; Salisbury Crags and Arthur's Seat; Duddingston village; Duddingston Loch; Innocent Railway Path.

The pubs: Sheep Heid Inn, Auld Hoose

Links: to walk 13

Arthur's Seat dominates the skyline of Edinburgh — rising to 820' (250m) and offering panoramic views in all directions. Surrounding the extinct volcano there's the extensive Holyrood Park with a variety of lower-level routes suitable for walking and cycling, so you don't have to be super fit to enjoy this route. The goal is the conservation village of Duddingston which still manages to retain some or its rural charm and feels much more rural and remote from the city centre than it is. The Sheep Heid Inn at Duddingston is a classic old Scottish inn of great antiquity and character, whilst birdwatchers should take their binoculars and detour to Duddingston Loch. The return to the city is along the interesting Innocent Railway Path, although there is a bus 'escape route' if you've had enough at Duddingston!

Salisbury Crags and the Radical Road

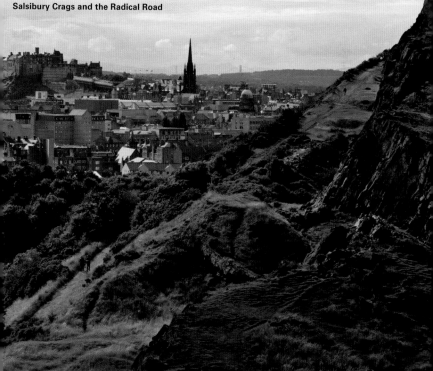

This is a very suitable circuit for a bicycle although you'll need to take Queen's Drive as far as Dunsapie Loch, and dismount down Jacob's Ladder. There's a good cycle path alongside the road as far as the first section under Sailsbury Crags.

Start at Holyrood Palace, accessible from the city centre by No. 36 bus from Waverley Bridge, or via the route detailed in walk 5 from the High Street/North Bridge junction. Follow the road to the right past the Scottish Parliament buildings and the new Dynamic Earth centre with a great view of Salisbury Crags ahead. Our route follows the Radical Road (see box), the rising slope at the foot of the vertical crags, above the grassy scree slope. The start of the route, almost directly across the Queen's Drive, the motor road encircling the whole Arthur's Seat massif, is pretty steep although the views are rewarding. Pause for breath and pick out some of the landmarks: the Castle on its crag is prominent of course, along with the sloping tail on which the Old Town is built. The modern flats of Dumbiedykes occupy the left foreground while beyond Holyrood is the port of Leith, and further

DUDDINGSTON LOCH

Duddingston Loch and bird sanctuary extends to about 20 acres in size but is very shallow with a maximum depth of only 10' (3m). The loch is popular with birdwatchers, with many species inhabiting the area, including wintering wildfowl, heron, water rail, tufted duck, mute swan and great crested grebe. There are also a number of nationally and locally scarce plants on the reserve. The loch has also given up some treasures: in 1778 over 50 Late Bronze Age weapons were dredged out and are now held by the National Museums of Scotland.

right the Hibernian football stadium (look for the green roof). Meadowbank sports stadium with its floodlights is further right still.

Pass the abandoned quarries further along and at the end of Salisbury Crags the Radical Road slopes down to a junction of paths by the road, under the steep western face of Arthur's Seat. If you are climbing the hill bear left into the obvious valley or *col* to the left, the Piper's Walk, and keep on this good path as it curves uphill and round to the right through some crags before another well-worn track to the

Holyrood
Palace

Scottish
Parliament

CANONGATE

HOLYROOD ROAD

QUEEN'S DRIVE

Our Dynamic
Earth

QUEEN'S DRIVE

St Margaret's
Loch

Holyrood

Whinny
Hill

Park

QUEEN'S DRIVE

RADICAL ROAD

Hunter's Bog

Dunsapie
Loch

Dunsapie
Hill

DUDDINGS

Salisbury
Crags

JACOBS LADDER

2

Arthur's
Seat

1

ST LEONARD'S STREET

HOLYROOD PARK RD

QUEEN'S DRIVE

Samson's Ribs

Duddingston
Loch

Key

▬ ▬ ▬ ▬ Walk route

• • • • • • Alternative route

right leads to the summit. Unless you're an experienced hill walker the ascent is best left alone in mist. From the summit with its fine views all around partially retrace your steps and pick up a good straight path heading due east down the mostly gentle slopes to reach the Queen's Drive road close to the Dunsapie Loch car park which you'll see on the way down.

The alternative option at the col is to follow the usually fairly quiet section of the Queen's Drive around the southern side of the hill. This climbs steadily at first to offer excellent views across the city and over Duddingston Loch which we shall be passing later. The Jacob's Ladder path down to Duddingston village leaves the road a short distance south of the car park (just at the end of the sharp left hand bend) where you'll see steps dropping down towards a wall. Approaching from Arthur's Seat, simply walk back down the road to the right from the car park a short distance. The path then follows the wall down a long but well-constructed and easy to negotiate staircase which satisfyingly deposits you right at the edge of the conservation village of Duddingston. This is the point where you might want to make the short detour to the shore of Duddingston Loch by crossing pretty much directly over the road in front of you. Otherwise turn immediately left at the bottom of Jacob's Ladder into a short alleyway which brings you right out opposite the **Sheep Heid Inn** 🛈. This is a real gem of a pub which oozes character throughout, and claims to be Scotland's oldest, dating back to 1360. Certainly the interior can't have changed much in the last few decades – there are several comfortable wood-panelled drinking areas arranged around the semi-circular bar counter. The walls and window-sills are covered in all sorts of genuine clutter (as opposed to the mock bookshelves etc that appear in made-over Irish and other chain pubs). This is also a pub that knows something about its beer, and you can expect three regularly changing ales on the counter although if you're lucky enough to be here over Easter when the pub's Beer Festival takes place in the central courtyard, you may well end up having a long session! The place also prides itself on its food which is available until 8pm weekdays and 9pm weekends. At the rear is a skittle alley, a rarity these days.

Photo of the Sheep Heid 1935

Come out of the pub and turn left down the lane past the car park and turn left at the 'T' junction by the attractive old Kirk, one of Scotland's oldest in uninterrupted use. Walk down past some handsome villas to the main road. This is where you will pick up a bus if you want to abort here and return to the city centre: cross the road and the half hourly service 42 takes 25 minutes back to Waverley Bridge. Otherwise follow the road right for the best part of half a mile and as it curves around the edge of the loch (see box). There is a footpath short cut which heads off into the woodland along a fence on the sharp right hand bend beyond the school, which brings you out almost at the start of the Innocent Railway Path which you'll otherwise pick up on the main road in 8-10 minutes walk.

You won't miss the turning to the right onto the Innocent Railway Path, about half a mile from Duddingston. The Innocent Railway was so called because when it was built, very early in the railway era around 1830, it was a horse drawn line as steam engines were still considered new-fangled and decidedly dangerous. It was a short branch off the Edinburgh to Dalkeith line, constructed to carry goods, especially coal from mines around Dalkeith, and it ran into a terminus at St. Leonards, very close to the Auld Hoose (below). What took the promoters off guard was the meteoric rise in popularity and public acceptance of the railway and this route was soon a successful passenger line. Where we join the route, now a cycle and foot path, you immediately cross what looks like an unexciting little bridge over the tiny Braid Burn, but it's in fact one of the earliest surviving cast iron beam bridges of its type. The railway's other claim to fame is one of Britain's first railway tunnels, which is still part of the public path, stretching about 400 yards under the southern edge of Holyrood Park. The path leads close to the southern shore of the loch (but with no public access from this side) for almost a mile before arriving at the well lit tunnel; if you don't fancy the walk through the tunnel there's a path climbing to join the road and you can follow the traffic on the verge to St. Leonard's Street instead. Emerging from the tunnel follow the cycle route through the new housing estate which occupies the old St. Leonards goods yard. At the end of this turn left up the lane (cycle route signs) to join St. Leonards Street by the police offices. Don't worry if you emerge onto the main road too soon – it's just further to walk down to the right, until you reach the **Auld Hoose**  at No. 23.

Sheep Heid Inn

Billing itself as the 'Southside's only alternative pub' this atmospheric tenement bar in the student area is primarily aimed at a young crowd but I had no trouble getting in, and with three well-kept ales you may want to linger. Caledonian Deuchars IPA and, unusually, Wychwood Hobgoblin are the regulars, joined by a rotating guest from a Scottish micro-brewery. There's also Addlestone's cask cider and quite a few others in bottle if you like that sort of stuff. Seating is arranged on floorboards around the horseshoe servery, whilst the walls are adorned with a mixture of photos of old Edinburgh and far newer gig posters. Be warned that loud music is a possibility, from the 'eclectic jukebox with an awesome selection of Metal, Punk, Rock, and Goth'… to quote the website. Finally it's worth knowing after your long walk back from Duddingston that the place offers highly rated food and plenty of it until late (9.30pm weekdays, 8pm Sundays) with the menu available on the website.

To return to the city centre it's best to cut through to Clerk Street via Crosscausway (left out the pub and left again) where there are buses galore from the opposite side of the road. ▶**LINK**◀

PUB INFORMATION

1 **Sheep Heid Inn**
43-45 The Causeway,
Edinburgh, EH15 3QA
0131 661 7974
www.sheepheid.co.uk
Opening Hours: 11-11 (11.30 Fri & Sat)
CAMRA Regional Inventory

2 **Auld House**
23/25 St Leonards St,
Edinburgh, EH8 9QN
0131 668 2934
www.theauldhoose.co.uk
Opening Hours: 12 (12.30 Sun)-12.45am)

The skittle alley at the Sheep Heid Inn

▶**LINK**◀ Walk 13 **Into the Southside** (page 75) pick up walk 13 on Clerk Street, just after the *Dagda Bar*.

Over the Blackford and Braid Hills to Mortonhall and Morningside

WALK INFORMATION

Start: North Gate to Blackford Hill Local Nature Reserve (LNR)

Finish: Morningside

Access: Bus No. 41 from Princes Street

Distance: 5 miles (8 km)

Key attractions: Blackford Hill LNR, Royal Observatory visitor centre Blackford Hill*, Braid Burn, Hermitage of Braid visitor centre

The pubs: Stable Bar, Buckstone Bistro, Bennets Bar

Links: none

*Currently closed for maintenance (early 2010) – check www.roe.ac.uk/vc or ring 0131 668 8404

This is a proper walk, considerably longer than all the others in this book with the exception of the Balerno, and North Berwick to Gullane routes. It's one of my favorite Edinburgh walks, taking in two of the city's 'seven hills' and visiting the charming Braid Burn. Blackford Hill in particular offers a range of habitats including 150 acres of mixed mature woodland, scrub and grassland, as well as the Braid Burn and small wetland areas with a rich diversity of wildlife – so if you're that way inclined it's worth taking the binoculars. In addition you can climb the summit for an excellent view and then stroll across to the nearby Royal Observatory to help you work up a thirst. I recommend packing a flask and a snack in your rucksack since even without this detour the first pub is a good distance from the start.

Edinburgh's excellent bus network means that it's possible to shorten this route in several ways if you don't fancy the full 5 miles or so for the whole walk. Briefly those options are to take a bus to Mortonhall and the Stable Bar and thereby cut out the first couple of miles; alternatively to walk up to the Stable Bar and finish at Mortonhall and either take a bus home or bus it round to the Morningside pubs; or to cut out the Stable Bar section (which would be a pity) and follow the Braid Burn right the way down emerging close to the Buckstone Bistro... Whichever option you choose you can be sure of an enjoyable walk and one where you can justly feel that you have earned your liquid refreshment.

Salisbury Crags and Arthur's Seat from Braid Hills Drive

To start at the northern entrance to Blackford Hill, take a No. 41 bus from the city centre (Princes Street, Waverley Bridge or George IV Bridge close to the Royal Mile) but with the destination of Craighouse and NOT King's buildings. Alight at the gateway on Charterhall Road (ask the driver for the correct stop).

Walk in by the gatehouse – there's a helpful map just inside the entrance – and bear right past Blackford Pond to follow the excellent path which climbs steadily but not too steeply uphill past some attractively sited allotments on the steep south-facing

The Hermitage of Braid

hillside. You arrive at a junction of paths where the right turn leads back downhill towards a car park and the left turn climbs steeply up towards the mast and beyond, the Observatory, at the top of Blackford Hill. If you're feeling energetic this is an option you may wish to take up, returning

Key

― ― ― ― Walk route

• • • • • • Detour

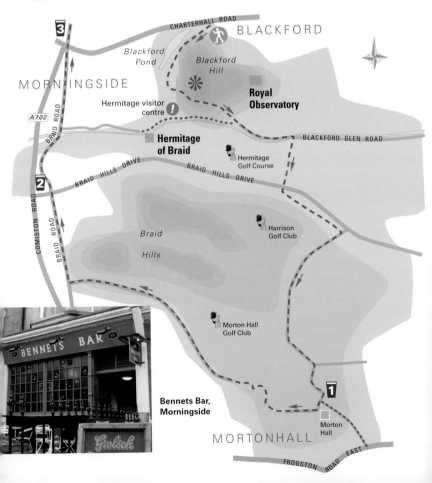

the same way afterwards. Our route continues ahead with the pathway bearing gently around to the left and leveling out with the steep slopes of the hill on your left and an equally steep drop through woodland on your right. When the path starts to lose height keep on the main track which drops steadily (and indeed at the end quite steeply) down to meet the stream, the Braid Burn, by a footbridge. This is a very pleasant spot to open your flask if you have one! Here we want to turn left downstream but a strongly recommended option is to detour upstream for about 10 minutes through the attractive wooded valley to the Hermitage of Braid. This picturesque two-storeyed villa in a mixture of Medieval and Classical styles was built in 1785 by the architect, Robert Burn, in the wooded valley of the Braid Burn. It's now a visitor centre in the care of Edinburgh City Council. This is also the route that you can take if you wish to cut out the lengthy but attractive walk up to the Stable Bar at Mortonhall; in which case simply continue beyond the Hermitage on the tarred road which will bring you out on the main road just north of the Buckstone Bistro.

Back at the footbridge, continue downstream (signposted to Blackford Glen road) where the landscape becomes more open – the crag overlooking the path further down is Agassiz rock, which has a special place in geological history. In 1840 Swiss Geologist Louis Agassiz noticed that this rock was polished and grooved by the passage of ice across its surface. His observation here marked the first recognition in the world of the presence of ancient ice sheets and initiated our understanding of how ancient glaciers shaped the landscape. Due to its great geological importance the rock is now a Site of Special Scientific Interest (SSSI). Just beyond, cross the river on the footbridge (signed Howe Dean Path) and gird your loins for a fairly stiff pull uphill to join the Braid Hills Drive at the top. Cross straight over and go through the kissing gate and onto the edge of the golf course.

Before bearing sharp left on a good pathway running parallel to the road through the bracken and gorse take a well-earned rest. Provided the weather is good you'll be rewarded with an excellent and extensive view right across the city and the Firth of Forth, with Arthur's Seat and Salisbury Crags very prominent. In about 400 yards the path brings you out onto the Braid Hills bridlepath by the entrance to the golf course. Bear right here, and now it's simply a matter of following this lane uphill southwards. On your right the land rises over the golf course towards the summit of the Braid Hills; whilst to your left good views open out to the east: the prominent but distant conical hill is North Berwick Law. The lane becomes more rural in character as it reaches Meadowhead farm. About 300 yards beyond Meadowhead we bear right by a lodge and signpost and stroll downhill towards Morton Hall which soon comes into view through the woodland. Walk down towards the car park and the house ignoring the footpath heading off on the right. However it's not the impressive house that we are primarily interested in, but the stable block on the left – for through the archway, and well-deserved after a long but rewarding plod is the first pub of the day:

Blackford Glen

the **Stable Bar** 1 . Converted to pub use about 30 years ago this is a real rural gem on the edge of the city. The attractive and spacious bar is dominated by the enormous stone fireplace which in winter is stacked with huge logs. There is a dining room leading off if you want a formal sit-down meal but the first thoughts surely will be to sample one of the three locally-brewed real ales on offer here – Caledonian Deuchars IPA, and Stewart brewery's 80/- and Copper Cascade. Remember if you get too comfortable and end up unable or unwilling to walk much further you can abort here and walk the short distance to the main road (ask for directions at the bar if you're unsure of the route) to catch a No. 11 (across the road, heading right) either all the way to the city or into Morningside close to Bennets Bar.

For those hardy souls who are doing things properly however, emerge from the courtyard, when the time comes, and bear left down towards the house. Take the path down to the right in front of the house (signposted Buckstone) and follow this through the trees, and then as it curves to the right around a semi-derelict wall and appears to peter out you should see a clear path heading left uphill through the scrub and trees. Take this path, go through a gate and you'll quickly join a very good wide track. Bear left (signed Braid Road and Mounthooly Loan), and then keeping right at the fork of paths shortly afterwards (Braid Road) with the fence on your immediate right simply follow this path for the best part of a mile with open country and woodland on your right hand side, and modern houses and a school through the trees on your left. Eventually you join the road very close to yet another golf club house. The sport has annexed pretty well the whole of the Braid Hills. If you are done in by now you can cheat and take a bus (Nos 11 and 15) into Morningside (but be aware they run on the parallel main road and you need to walk down to the left to get to the bus stop) otherwise simply turn right and walk on this road for about 500 yards, and just where it bends round to the left you'll spot on your left the **Buckstone Bistro** 2 . As the name implies this is an unapologetically modern affair, built adjacent to the Victorian Braid Hills Hotel. Lovers of traditional pubs may wince but after a long walk you will be ready for a drink, and the good news is that there are three real ales available on the bar: Deuchars IPA, Greene King IPA and that very distinctive citrus straw-colored beer from Harviestoun, Bitter & Twisted. Meals are available throughout the day until 9.30pm, which is worth remembering as your next and last stop does not offer food.

Leaving the Buckstone, simply continue along the Braid Road as it curves around and then straightens its course for another half a mile until it joins the main road in the centre of Morningside, by a large pub, the *Morningside Glory*. A very short distance further on just over the railway bridge lookout for **Bennets Bar** 3 on the corner of the next left hand turning. In contrast to the last stop this is a really traditional local and something of a Morningside institution which, until recently had been in the same family for many years. It has a plain and satisfying interior with red banquette seating along the walls. Best all is the wide selection of ales: Deuchars IPA of course, Timothy Taylor Landlord and up to four changing guest beers. On the walls is an interesting display of photographs of old Edinburgh including an interesting picture of the of original Bennets close to Waverley station; whilst in good weather you can sit outside at the pavement tables and gaze at life in this rather genteel suburb. Just about all the buses passing here will take you back into the city centre so you won't have long to wait.

PUB INFORMATION

1 Stable Bar
50 Mortonhall Gate, Edinburgh,
EH16 6TJ
0131 664 0773
www.mortonhall.co.uk/home/
bar/stablebar.htm
Opening Hours: 11 (12.30
Sun)-11

2 Buckstone Bistro
134 Braid Rd, Edinburgh, EH10 6JD
0131 447 8888

www.braidhillshotel.co.uk/
BuckstoneBarBistro.asp
Opening Hours: 11 (12.30
Sun)-11

3 Bennets Bar
1 Maxwell St, Edinburgh,
EH10 5HT
0131 447 1903
Opening Hours: 11-midnight;
12.30-10 Sun
CAMRA Regional Inventory

Water of Leith Walkway: Colinton Dell and Balerno from Slateford

WALK INFORMATION

Start: Slateford, by the Water of Leith Visitor Centre

Finish: Balerno

Access: Trains from Waverley, or No. 44 bus from Waverley Bridge

Distance: 5.8 miles (9.2km)

Key attractions: Water of Leith Visitor Centre, Craiglockhart and Colinton Dells, Redhall walled garden, Colinton conservation village, Malleny garden Balerno

The pubs: Spylaw Tavern, Juniper Green Inn, Kinleith Arms, Riccarton Arms, Grey Horse

Links: None

Craiglockhart and Colinton Dells make up an extensive area of woodland and open space along the Water of Leith. The first part of the walk is along the most attractive section of the Water of Leith Walkway, where the river is at its most unspoilt in the vicinity of the city. The demise of the railway and mills hereabouts has left one important legacy – a good path which you can follow way beyond Colinton to the village of Balerno, with the river your companion throughout. There are plenty of pubs to refresh you on the way, and all offer food so you're spoilt for choice. A good route too for lovers of industrial archaeology with evidence of mill remains to be seen in several places. Thanks to the ridiculously frequent buses you can abort the walk at just about any point and be whisked back to the city.

An old mill house by the waterside near Juniper Green

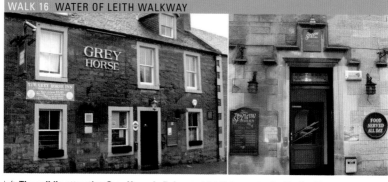

left: **The solidly attractive Grey Horse in Balerno** right: **Entrance to the Spylaw Tavern**

Start this walk at Water of Leith Visitor Centre at Slateford, opposite the Dell Inn. This is accessible either by train from Waverley (ten minutes, then five minutes' walk to the Water of Leith) or the 44 bus which follows the route closely throughout. The visitor centre, under the shadow both of the railway viaduct and the union canal aqueduct, makes a great place to start this walk: it's open from 10am daily. You can also pick up an inexpensive map of the Walkway which would make an informative accompaniment and enhance your enjoyment of the route. More information at www.waterofleith.org.uk/centre

The modern **Dell Inn** [7] across the road has an attractive riverside garden (and real ale in the shape of two rotating guests; one only during winter months) but it's probably one to leave for then way home if you want to visit, there is no shortage of hostelries on this route! Just adjacent (left as you face the inn) is the entrance to Craiglockart and Colinton Dells, a linear ribbon of woodland and parkland which accompanies the river for over a mile. The instructions are simple really; follow a path and keep the river in view – it's pretty difficult to get lost in here. There's a lot to see though – for one thing it's a great natural habitat for birds and waterside wildlife. The range of trees here is wide too – ash, lime, elm, birch, willow and hawthorn, with oak, yew, holly, hornbeam, cedar, sweet chestnut and beech on the upper slopes. En route you might be tempted by Redhall walled garden on the opposite bank of the river (access

via footbridge). Currently the garden is successfully operated as an organic and therapeutic working garden for people with mental health issues; open until about 3.30pm on weekdays. On the same side of the river is the old railway track bed, now the cycle route, which could be used as a return route if you're only going as far as Colinton.

Close to the river on the path you'll pass a little domed building, built as a grotto, probably for the owner of Craiglockhart House in around 1830.

This stretch of the river valley was once home to numerous mills, and one of the more obvious is where the path eventually rises to join a small lane at Kates Mill – as it does you can spot a mill tail race on your right. This was a channel where water was returned to a stream, having been diverted through a mill wheel. Here at Kates Mill, according to the *Gazetteer of Scotland*, paper for the first Bank of Scotland banknotes was produced. Beyond the house are the remains of Redhall Mill (hidden by a wooden fence) where you'll pick a up the path running on a little footbridge across the leat or mill race and then running between this and the river for a short way, until you reach the impressive weir. Cross the river on the footbridge here and walk the remaining distance to Colinton where you ascend up some steps to a photogenic spot by the old Colinton Church and original old stone bridge over the river. The church, whilst attractive in its own right, is perhaps most notable

LANARK

A70

LANARK ROAD WEST

Water of Leith

for its churchyard, which contains the graves of philanthropist James Gillespie (see below) and Lewis Balfour, the grandfather of author and poet Robert Louis Stevenson. An iron mortsafe lies in the churchyard, used to protect newly buried bodies from the attentions of the 'Resurrectionists' or bodysnatchers who made money by selling bodies to the Edinburgh medical school.

The old village street of Colinton, now pleasantly free of through traffic, climbs steeply up from the valley and on the right towards the top is the **Spylaw Tavern** 1. An attractive frontage leads into a long narrow interior which at the rear has a garden area above the river. Freshly prepared food is served all day (there's an eating area towards the rear), washed down with the almost mandatory Caldeonian Deuchars IPA plus a changing guest.

If you're game for another pub here in Colinton, look for the steep wynd (Cuddies Lane) almost opposite the Spylaw Tavern which takes you up onto the main road above, where a short distance to your left is the **Colinton Inn** 6 where'll you'll find Caledonian Deuchars IPA and maybe a guest. There is a delightful terraced garden at the back downstairs. This is also the place to pick up the bus (routes 10 or 45) back into the city if you've had enough walking. It's also an option if you're heading back here, to walk back a different way along the old railway route which is now a cycleway (see below). Either way, take the path a few yards uphill from the Spylaw Tavern into Spylaw Park. Down here on the left is the handsome Spylaw House by the river. Built in 1773 it was the home of the philanthropist James Gillespie. Gillespie also had a snuff mill here, round the back where it didn't offend the polite architecture of the pedimented frontage and attractive curved double stair to the entrance. James Gillespie died a rich man in 1797 but left his money to found a 'Hospital for the

Maintenance of Aged Men and Women; and of a Free School for the Education of Poor Boys'.

The rail/cycle route is behind the wall on the right hand side of the parkland – a path leads up to it, and once Colinton station stood here. If you're heading back to Slateford (on the cycle path via the old rail route and later the canal towpath) turn right and follow the trail through the old railway tunnel, it's pretty much as simple as that. To carry on, bear left and soon you will cross the river then bear right at the signpost and here the path widens. Soon the Water of Leith is crossed again close to the site of West Colinton Mill which for part of its working life was turning out Scott's Porage Oats. The path once more picks up its close course along the riverbank. In about a kilometre you come to one of the largest weirs on the river, and immediately above it the new Edinburgh Bypass road. Here the path skirts a modern housing development. Beyond this and at the end of some derelict buildings close to a footbridge, a rough road zig-zags away from the river. Take this, for at the top you're yards away from your next stop, the **Juniper Green Inn** 2. Formerly known as the Railway Tavern, a name which became increasingly anachronistic now the line has been closed for so long, it's had a modern makeover outside. The landlord is welcoming and the place retains some character in the substantial old mahogany bar

SLATEFORD

COLINTON DELL

Kinleith
Arms

counter, fronted with an array of traditional bar stools, and a huge Usher's mirror on the wall. The four handpumps dispense a changing variety of ales although Caledonian Deuchars IPA is a regular. The good quality lunchtime meals are freshly prepared. Leaving the pub, turn right and stay on the road for about 200 yards for here is the **Kinleith Arms 3**. From the outside it's easier to appreciate the age of this slate-roofed stone inn. Inside it's been modernised beyond redemption save for a bit of stained glass in the windows. The central bar partially separates the former 'public' and 'lounge' areas, the latter given over largely to diners these days. The pub has now brought in a third cask ale, a rotating guest, to supplement the Deuchars IPA and Courage Directors Bitter, the latter being very popular with the regulars. Food is available lunchtimes until 2.30, and evenings until 8, and right through the day from Fridays until Sundays.

Again if you've had enough by now help is at hand in the shape of the mega-frequent 44 bus.

To get back to the walkway, look for the signed entry almost opposite which leads you quickly down via a slope and steps back to the riverside. Turn right. The trail crosses the river on a footbridge with an old mill cottage below, then ducks under a road bridge. A short distance along here stood Kinleith Mill, one of the largest mills on the river, employing about 400 people at its peak. It closed in 1966 and the site has been decaying quietly since, although is now awaiting redevelopment so it's fenced off and a bit messy just now. The impressive weir remains, along with the first section of the old mill race a little downstream.

If you're ready for further refreshment at Currie Kirk and old bridge beyond – the bridge is one of the oldest across the river – take the lane up to the main road, and as you climb you'll spot the **Riccarton Arms 4**. The long lounge bar in this one-time farmhouse is comfortable, with a carpeted floor apart from mosaic tiling around the servery. The two handpumps are occupied by… you guessed it, Deuchars IPA, Greene King, Old Speckled Hen; and a rotating guest, usually a darker, maltier beer. Home cooked food is on offer until 8pm, and if you miss your last bus home the place offers bed & breakfast with five bedrooms. Once again the bus stop is outside, but you're almost there now; don't give up at this stage! Back on the river it's now just over a mile to Balerno. The trail ends just short of the school, where you then follow the road down to the junction. It's then a left turn up into the part pedestrianised main street which leads uphill, and it's just here that the final port of call stands: the **Grey Horse 5**. This traditional eighteenth century house looks the part with a solid, no-nonsense stone façade. Inside, although modernised, the public bar retains character with wood panelling and a fine old Bernard's brewery mirror. The adjacent lounge offers banquette seats and comfortable surroundings. If you're arriving here at the end of a long tramp, don't worry: you can eat here whilst downing your ale, Deuchars IPA, Greene King Old Speckled Hen and a rotating guest, kept in good condition. The 44 bus stop for Edinburgh is at the top of the street, if you don't feel like walking back to Slateford…

PUB INFORMATION

1 Spylaw Tavern
27 Spylaw St, Colinton, EH13 0JT
0131 441 2783
www.spylawtavern.co.uk
Opening Hours: 11.30 (12 Sun)-11 (midnight Fri-Sun)

2 Juniper Green Inn
542 Lanark Rd, Juniper Green, EH14 5EL
0131 458 5395
Opening Hours: 12-11 Mon-Wed; 11-midnight Thu-Sat; 12.30-11 Sun

3 Kinleith Arms
604 Lanark Rd, Juniper Green, EH14 5EN
0131 453 3214
Opening Hours: 10am-1am

4 Riccarton Arms
198 Lanark Rd West, Currie, EH14 5NX
0131 449 2230
www.thericcartonarms.co.uk
Opening Hours: 11-11 (midnight Fri & Sat)

5 Grey Horse
16-18 Main St, Balerno, EH14 7EH
0131 449 2888
www.greyhorseinn.co.uk
Opening Hours: 10 (12.30 Sun)-1am

TRY ALSO:

6 Colinton Inn
12 Bridge Rd, Colinton, EH13 0LQ
0131 441 3218
www.colintoninn.co.uk
Opening Hours: 12 (12.30 Sun)-11 (midnight Wed & Thu; 1am Fri; 12.30am Sat)

7 Dell Inn
27 Lanark Rd, Edinburgh, EH14 1TG
0131 443 9991
Opening Hours: 11-11

We are proud to serve locally-brewed real ale
CAMRA accredited 2009

Portobello: Edinburgh-on-Sea

WALK INFORMATION

Start: Brunstane rail station

Finish: Portobello

Access: Trains to Brunstane, buses No.15 or 26 to Joppa

Distance: 2.8 miles (4.5km)

Key attractions: Portobello promenade, Portobello Swim Centre Victorian Turkish baths

The pubs: Ormelie Tavern, Dalriada, Espy, Three Monkeys

Links: to walk 14 and 18

Portobello was an area of barren heath beside the Firth of Forth until the late eighteenth century. The name comes from a house built in about 1750 by George Hamilton, a sailor involved in the Battle of Puerto Bello in Panama in 1739 in which six British warships attacked and captured the Spanish-run port. Incidentally this is the same skirmish which led to the renaming of the famous West London street. A pottery industry developed and some elegant villas sprung up after 1770. In the early nineteenth century Portobello became popular as a seaside holiday town – the first bathing machines were reported in 1795, and a pier was built in 1871 by Thomas Bouch, designer of the ill-fated Tay Railway Bridge. Like a lot of resorts, Portobello is well-worn and has no doubt seen better days, but on a warm day or evening it's still got that seaside magic and you could do a lot, lot worse than watch the sun set from the garden of the Dalriada, right on the seafront.

The Portobello seafront from Joppa

Dalriada bar

For the whole circuit, take the train to Brunstane (the Newcraighall service) – the first stop after Waverley. If you prefer to omit the inland section, simply catch a bus – services 15 and 26 are the best options. They will take you down to the Eastfield turning circle on the Joppa promenade – and pick up the route below. Leave the platform by the front of the train and join the road – almost opposite you'll see a signed path 'Brunstane Burn Walkway' which then ducks down to the left, after 50 yards, onto a good path. This joins the burn and follows the course

of the stream, swinging right after a few minutes to bridge the stream and crossing under another railway line and past a graveyard on the opposite bank. When you join the edge of a housing estate and reach a junction of paths continue ahead on the Brunstane pathway to join the main road. Turn left and in a hundred yards or so, ignoring the bypass road running off to the left, cross here and take the coast road (signed Portobello) along what becomes the promenade at Eastfield before the Portobello esplanade is reached at Joppa.

The seafront curves away to the west, towards Leith, and soon the traffic-free promenade parts company with the road. But leave the coast for a moment as the first pub on the route is just a few yards along the Joppa Road at this point. The **Ormelie Tavern** 1 hasn't got the most attractive exterior you'll see, but inside it's a pleasant pub with a long bar counter and a decent gantry dating from 1904 well-stocked with a dazzling array of malt whiskies. It has four handpumps offering Caledonian Deuchars IPA, Stewart 80/- and two changing guest beers, which include offerings from south of the border.

Leaving the Ormelie, continue to the next corner (Morton Street) and head down the short distance to the Promenade which you'll follow for most of the rest of the route. Views out

Key

■ ■ ■ ■ ■ Walk route

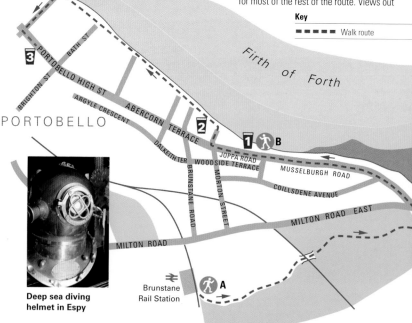

Deep sea diving helmet in Espy

across the Forth include Inchkeith island a few miles offshore, and the Fife coast beyond. The promenade here is particularly attractive with a very maritime-looking terrace to your right and a couple of surviving large houses looking out over the traffic free walkway; happily, one of these is now a pub. **Dalriada** 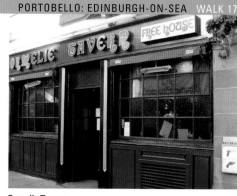 must, in good weather, be one of the best-sited entries in this book. It's a handsome detached villa with seating in the front garden. As you walk in, you're greeted by an original fireplace and tiled floor. There are three drinking areas served from the classy marble-topped bar, four if you count the garden. Live music occurs at the weekends. This pub was runner-up in the local CAMRA 2008 Pub of the Year competition. Watch out for the restricted winter hours though – it's closed all day Monday and Tuesday, and open evenings only from 5 on other weekdays...

Continue down the Promenade towards

Ormelie Tavern

the centre of Portobello. The view here was once dominated by Portobello power station, but this, along with an outdoor swimming pool next door, was demolished in the late 1970s to be replaced by the indoor bowling centre and the pavilion which you can see ahead. You can still swim at the restored Victorian Turkish baths that you pass on your left – now run as the Portobello Swim Centre – housed in a handsome redbrick building facing the beach. Featuring four rooms of varying temperatures and a cold plunge pool, they're one of only three surviving Turkish baths in Scotland.

Keep walking until you arrive at the corner of Bath Street where you'll find a handsome four storey Victorian

Dalriada occupies and enviable location on the seafront

left: **Comfortable corner in the Three Monkeys** right: **Espy occupies a handsome tenement block**

block, with at the foot, the **Espy** 3. A pub that has been made over and taken well upmarket, the Espy (which rhymes with 'pee' rather than 'pie' and is apparently a short version of 'esplanade') offers attentive table service and bonhomie dispensed, on our last visit at least, by cheery Australian bar staff. There are two cask ales: Deuchars IPA and a rotating guest, although beer isn't the main focus here and the wine list is far longer. You can pick up something to eat here from a wide menu which is available on the website. The interior is modern, and you can enjoy good views out to sea beyond the punters promenading outside.

And now for something more traditional… for your last pub, walk a little further down the prom and beyond a little playground take one of the two streets heading away from the sea, Beach Lane or Figgate Lane; and follow up to the High Street. Across the road and just a little to the right you'll spot the **Three Monkeys** 4. Dark wood, bench seats and that indefinable ingredient of 'pubbiness' prevail here, despite the name change from the ultra traditional Plough Inn. Space is well used with a little semi separate snug at the front and small stage area where events aimed at bringing in more punters are held, like open mic sessions on Mondays and live bands on Saturday nights. Beer is well kept and the young licensee is trying new guests along with a Stewart beer as a regular. Light lunches are served. ▶ **LINK** Returning to the city centre buses 15 and 26 from the stop close by offer the fastest and most direct route.

PUB INFORMATION

1 Ormelie Tavern
44 Joppa Rd, Edinburgh, EH15 2ET
0131 669 3323
Opening Hours: 11–midnight
(12.45am Fri & Sat); 12.30-11 Sun

2 Dalriada
77 Promenade, Edinburgh, EH15 2EL
0131 454 4500
www.dalriadabar.co.uk
Opening Hours: 12 (12.30 Sun; 5
Jan & Feb)-midnight

3 Espy
62-64 Bath St, Edinburgh, EH15 1HF
0131 669 0082
www.the-espy.com
Opening Hours: 12-2am

4 Three Monkeys
87 Portobello High St, Edinburgh,
EH15 1AW
0131 669 7155|
www.thethreemonkeys.co.uk
Opening Hours: 11.30am-
midnight

▶ **LINK** Walk 18 **Leith Old and New** (page 97) Take bus 21 from the Three Monkeys to the foot of Leith Walk (a ten minute ride) to pick up walk 18.

▶ **LINK** Walk 14 **Holyrood Park, Duddingston Loch and the Innocent Railway Path** (page 79) Cross the road and catch half hourly service 42 for an even shorter ride to Duddingston and the *Sheep Heid Inn*.

Beyond the Fringe

top: **Tyneside Tavern exterior** bottom: **Stained glass at the Feuars Arms**

Leith Old and New

WALK INFORMATION

Start: Foot of Leith Walk

Finish: Starbank Inn

Access: Buses 10, 12, 16, 22 and 25 from Princes Street/St. Andrew Square

Distance: 2.5 miles (4km)

Key attractions: Trinity House, Leith Links, Lamb's House

The pubs: Shore Bar, Teuchter's Landing, Malt & Hops, Starbank Inn

Links: None

The most important thing to remember about Leith is that it isn't Edinburgh! Leithers have always been fiercely independent, and never voted for amalgamation with their larger neighbour — but of course the rapid decline of the old port and the associated industries, and the regeneration of the place, has brought a lot of new faces into Leith. Our walk takes in a good deal of the history of Leith as well as visiting its best pubs.

Trinity House, Leith

Start at the foot of Leith Walk — buses down the Leith Walk from central Edinburgh are numerous and very frequent. Pub architecture enthusiasts might want to at least peer in at the *Central Bar* at the bottom of Leith Walk: it features in *Scotland's True Heritage Pubs*, but sadly offers no real ale.

Cross to the pedestrianised New Kirkgate with its spiky Narwhal Monument. The now-demol-ished railway station across the street featured in the 1996 film of Irvine Welsh's *Trainspotting*. It's important to remember that Leith was Scotland's principal port until the rise of Glasgow. Nowhere epitomises that more than Trinity House at No. 99 Kirkgate, which has been called perhaps the finest museum of shipping in Scotland. The gravitas of the architecture is also a real treat after the dismal concrete shops of New Kirkgate. It was

Starbank Inn, Newhaven

Malt & Hops

from the Knights. William Wallace may well have stayed here too.

Walking through the peaceful graveyard with its lovely trees you will come to a gate on the far side. (If the graveyard route is closed walk a little further down and cut through via Coalfield Lane). Cross through here and go over Constitution Street and into Links Lane, from here you are at the corner of Leith Links. This, not St. Andrews – as Leithers will quickly tell you – is the real home of golf. The game here dates back to 1457 when it was run by the Honourable Company of Edinburgh Golfers (then called 'The Gentleman Golfers').

Follow John's Place along the Links to the crossroads, and turn left into Queen Charlotte Street with its handsome houses, to re-cross Constitution Street taking the second right into Water Street. Difficult to miss a little way down on the left is the Grade A listed Lamb's House, an impressive mid 17th century merchant's house, probably the finest in the town at the time. There's some evidence that Mary Queen of Scots, who landed at Leith on 19 August 1561 after returning from France, stayed briefly on a house on this site. Sadly at the time of writing it's looking very sorry for itself, although the very latest is that it is rumoured to have been bought and about to be revamped. Let's hope so. We're now approaching the heart of old Leith, and fittingly close to our first pub. Continue down the lane and as it bends sharply right, take the wide pedestrian alleyway through to the main road, Bernard Street, pretty well opposite the *Carriers Quarters*, an interesting

Key

━ ━ ━ ━ Walk route

originally founded as a hospice for mariners, paid for by a levy on goods landed at the port. The classical Georgian style of the current building dates from a rebuild in 1816, and it has a marvelous interior which is worth seeing in its own right, quite apart from the maritime exhibits. Tours must be booked in advance – the phone number is 0131 554 3289.

Across the street South Leith Parish Church has links with the Knights Templar who also had a hospice on the site. The first definite royal link with South Leith Parish Church is in 1327 with Robert the Bruce: according to court records he came to Leith to receive treatment for leprosy old pub into which you may wish to venture.

Anyway the route takes us to the left here and down to the traffic lights by the Water of Leith. Turn right here by the Granary Bar (which does a decent coffee) into the Shore, with the harbour across the street. You're right in the centre of historic Leith here, and a few yards along on your right is a plaque commemorating the King's Landing. In August 1822, King George IV landed where you're standing – the first visit from a monarch for nearly 200 years. Government ministers had pressed the King to bring forward a proposed visit to Scotland, to divert him from diplomatic intrigue at the Congress of the Nations in Vienna. The visit was a success and the kilt – banned in Scotland by the government after the Jacobite Rebellion of 1745, was, for the first time, developed as the national dress of Scotland – the starting point of the 'tartanification' of Scottish culture, enthusiastically cultivated by Walter Scott to try and improve the monarch's image in Scotland.

From the plaque make your way further along the Shore to the **Shore Bar 1** on your right. This bar has been taken firmly upmarket and focuses upon gastro type food, but you can get a drink here, usually Deuchars IPA and Greene King Abbot. It's pretty small inside but quite nicely refurbished, and if you're here during the day you might even be lucky enough to get a seat. If you're a cask ale fan just take a half pint here and save the serious drinking for the next two stops…

Carry on along the Shore: across the courtyard by Malmasion Hotel (which is a former seamen's home) is a bench with a statue of a man sitting down and a harpoon in the corner. This commemorates (if that's the right word) the association of Leith with whaling – and with Christian Salvesen, once the world's largest whaling company, who were based here in Leith.

Cross the mouth of the water of Leith by the iron Victoria Bridge which once carried trains into the port. If you feel like it you might detour

Hidden oasis – South Leith churchyard

across the road briefly to look at what's left of the Port of Leith. Follow the roadway past the new Scottish Executive building – which stands on reclaimed land – up to Commercial Quay. This is the heart of the regenerated waterfront of Leith and there are some very expensive restaurants and bars here. If you've time, amble along by the restored bonded warehouses – these were where whisky which was received from distillers and brought here was bottled and kept until duty was paid. Either way, you'll not miss your next calling point, right on the waterside as you head into Dock Place at the near end of the warehouses.

Teuchters Landing 2. Formerly known as the Waterfront Wine Bar, the new name invokes the lowland Scottish term for a Highlander, or rural migrant, so presumably it's not a reference to George IV! The interior has a smaller traditional bar at the front and a larger restaurant beyond, and the conservatory opens out onto a floating pontoon, so this is the only entry in this book where you can walk on water. Although the wine list dominates and there may be a few of Leith's affluent newcomers in evidence, the beer drinker isn't forgotten: expect Caledonian Deuchars IPA, Timothy Taylor Landlord, and the excellent straw coloured Ossian from Inveralmond.

View from the Starbank Tavern across the Firth of Forth to the mountains of Stirlingshire

King's Wark

Leaving Teuchters, head up Dock Street back to the main road. Turn left and you're back at the river bridge by the junction of Bernard Street and the Shore. Time for another drink, and we're now heading for Leith's foremost real ale pub, the **Malt & Hops** 3 which is a few doors to the right along the Shore at No. 45. One of my favourites in the Edinburgh region, the Malt & Hops has survived the influx of new money into Leith remarkably well, and still has its intimate dark atmosphere, with all sorts of knik-knaks festooned from walls and ceiling but more importantly eight handpumps dispensing a changing range of interesting beers including some rare one-offs and new brews – so you may even spot some beer scoopers in here. There's a full lunch menu from 12-2 Wednesday to Friday, snacks at other times. If your time is your own, you'd be mad not to want to spend a good bit of it in here. The coal fire is a welcome complement to the cosy atmosphere inside this gem of a pub.

The last 'official' pub stop on the route is best reached by bus – number 16 outside the pub across the street in the Silverknowes direction. If you want to stay in Leith and drink more, try the **King's Wark** 5, the handsome pub on the corner of the Shore and Bernard Street,

which offers real ales (Caledonian beers and a guest) and a more expensive food menu; and/ or the **Roseleaf** 6, Sandport Place, (walk the other way along the Shore and the road crossing the river is Sandport Place). Formerly the Black Swan and the birthplace of Edinburgh CAMRA, it's now firmly upmarket although it still looks very 'pubby' and has kept some of its old fittings. On offer is Deuchars IPA and a guest beer.

Otherwise (or afterwards) take the number 16 (if you're a purist you can simply walk along the coast road past the execrable Ocean Village shopperama – about 25 minutes) and alight in about a mile just after Newhaven harbour on the coastal Starbank Road (by the junction with Laverockbank Street). Here you're practically outside the **Starbank Inn** 4. This pleasantly sited inn with views over the Firth of Forth is fairly upmarket with another enticing selection of cask ales, including up to four rotating guests to complement the regulars, which include Timothy Taylor Landlord, Belhaven 80/- and Caledonian Deuchars IPA. There's a good range of reasonably priced meals on offer too, so it's a good place to end up after a satisfying day's mixture of culture and beer. Cheers!

Bus 16 in the opposite direction runs until 11.15pm back to the city.

PUB INFORMATION

1 Shore Bar
3 Shore, Leith, EH6 6QW
0131 553 5080
www.theshore.biz
Opening Hours: 12-1am

2 Teuchters Landing
1 Dock Pl, Leith, EH6 6LU
0131 554 7427
www.aroomin.co.uk/teuchters-landing
Opening Hours: 11am-1am

3 Malt & Hops
45 Shore, Leith, EH6 6QU
0131 555 0083
Opening Hours: 12 (12.30 Sun)-11 (midnight Wed & Thu; 1am Fri & Sat)

4 Starbank Inn
60-64 Laverockbank Rd, EH5 3BZ
0131 552 4141
www.starbankinn.co.uk

1 Shore Bar
Opening Hours: 11 (12.30 Sun)-11 (midnight Thu-Sat)

TRY ALSO:

5 King's Wark
36 Shore, Leith, EH6 6QU
0131 554 9260
Opening Hours: 12-11 (midnight Fri & Sat)

6 Roseleaf
23/24 Sandport Pl, Edinburgh, EH6 6EW
0131 476 5268
www.roseleaf.co.uk
Opening Hours: 10am-midnight (1am Fri & Sat)

Teuchters Landing is right on the waterside at Leith

The Esk Valley, Musselburgh and Prestonpans via the Coastal Path

WALK INFORMATION

Start: Monktonhall, by Musselburgh Golf Club

Finish: Prestonpans

Access: Bus No. 30 from Princes Street

Distance: to Musselburgh 3 miles (4.8 km); to Prestoungrange 6.2 miles (10 km)

Key attractions: Inveresk Lodge Garden, St. Michael's Kirk, Brunton Theatre, Levenhall Links and bird reserve, Prestongrange Industrial Museum, Prestonpans Murals

The pubs: The Volunteer Arms (Staggs), Levenhall Arms, Prestoungrange Gothenburg

Links: None

A long walk that can be broken into two sections – both full of interest – at Musselburgh, or walked end to end. The coastal section, following part of the John Muir Way, is best saved for a good day, but once you are in Musselburgh the useful 26 bus can be used to cut short the walking and visit the final two pubs. All the pubs on the route have features of interest, and you can expect a good range of well-kept beers. Staggs in Musselburgh has been a finalist in CAMRA's National Pub of the Year competition, while the Prestoungrange Gothenburg is a beautiful and lovingly-restored Art Nouveau gem which is now once again brewing its own very good beers. So it's no surprise that this is one of my favorite pub walks in the Edinburgh region.

It's worth making an early start, taking bus 30 from Princes Street/North Bridge to Mayfield Crescent on the outskirts of Musselburgh. Ask for the Jooglie Brig Hotel close by the entrance to Monktonhall Golf Course: the bus stop is just before the T junction with the main road. Continue down the main road, with open views over the hedge, and soon the road bends to the right past Monkton Hall, and just beyond, the entrance to the golf club. Now take Ferguson

The old bridge, Musselburgh

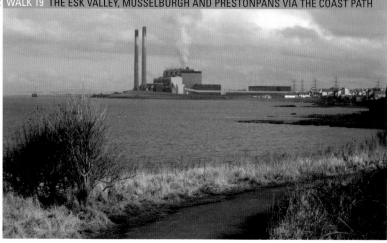

On the John Muir Way near Prestonpans

Drive, the last turning on the left before the railway bridge (cycleway sign). Follow the new houses down the drive with the golf course on the left and good views across to the prominent spire of Inveresk church, which we'll be visiting later. Under the railway bridge the scenery improves as you follow the tarred cycleway and swing left over the River Esk on a footbridge to bear left again on the good River Esk Path signed Musselburgh. The well-placed seat here would be a good riverside spot for your flask and

sandwiches, if you're so equipped.

Under the railway line once more, follow the pleasant riverside path before taking a signed footpath on the right as the river bends left; which leads up between walls into Inveresk village. The National Trust's Inveresk Lodge and garden is a short way down the road on the right, but our route turns left and continues straight ahead at the junction ahead to lead past the entrance to Inveresk House into the old conservation village and its charming old Kirk of St. Michael with its

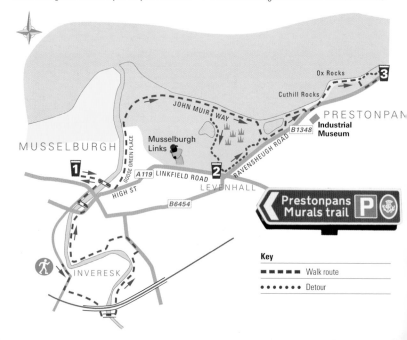

Staggs bar

splendid steeple. The formal churchyard is well worth a visit for its fine views back across to Edinburgh with Arthur's Seat very prominent, and across the Firth of Forth to the Fife coastline.

At the Kirk gates at the end of the lane there's a signed path leading you invitingly down a narrow walled alley back towards the river; it forks shortly – if you're cycling the route you'll need to opt for the steeper left hand slope but for walkers the right hand path is an attractive option running

gently down on a shady tree-lined terrace above the river before finally dropping down some steep stone steps to rejoin the path by the riverside.

Continue downstream passing The Falls, a very large weir which once powered several mills, large and small, as well as tanneries and other industries. The paths crosses the sluice and lade (or mill race) which still survives, but most of the large site on the right of the path and further on has been redeveloped. The Musselburgh Paper Mill operated here from the 1870s until its closure in 1971. Further downstream was the Net Mill where in 1820 James Paterson invented the mechanical net loom. Last and by no means least Bruntons internationally famous wire mill, founded in 1876, also occupied a huge site by the river. It was Bruntons who rigged the first airships, and many suspension bridges, including the Forth Road Bridge were cabled with wire from the Musselburgh plant. The iron footbridge you will soon pass downstream was built in 1923 to carry workers across the river to these mills.

Approaching the outskirts of town, the path

INVERESK

There has been a settlement on the site of this historic village since the Iron Age and the remains of a Roman settlement and fort can still be seen. Many of the stones on the outside walls of St. Michael's Kirk are of Roman origin. A small knoll known as Oliver's Mound and another mound in the kirkyard were both used by the Romans to command the approaches by land and sea and later by the Duke of Somerset in 1547 and Oliver Cromwell in 1650 for their cannon. Inveresk House was used by Oliver Cromwell as his headquarters, his horses being stabled in the church. Inveresk Lodge was built between 1683 and 1700. The gardens were gifted to the National Trust for Scotland in 1959 by Mrs Helen Brunton and are open to the public. See www.nts.org.uk/Property/35 for more details. The village has a remarkable collection of 18th and 19th century listed buildings, many having been owned by famous literary, legal and historical figures over the years and it is protected as part of an Outstanding Conservation Area.

St. Michael's Kirk, Inveresk

THE GOTHENBURG SYSTEM

The Gothenburg Public House movement originated in the Swedish city of Gothenburg in the 19th century in an attempt to control the consumption of alcohol. The city set up a Trust which controlled retail spirits licences, following an 1855 law forbidding the distillation of spirits at home. This trust aimed to control pubs and off-sales outlets so as to discourage excessive consumption of spirits. 5% of the profit of the trusts went to the shareholders with the remainder being used for community benefit. The Gothenburg system quickly spread, and in Scotland it was adopted mainly in mining communities of Fife and the Lothians as a means of discouraging miners from over indulging in the demon drink. The *Dean Tavern* in the old mining village of Newtongrange a few miles from Prestonpans is also still run on Gothenburg lines. The Prestonpans Goth still adheres to the Gothenburg principles by donating some of its profits to the Prestoungrange Art Festival.

The terrace path above the river at Inveresk

Don't be put off by the Tennents lager sign outside for this is a really excellent real ale destination, from the moment you enter via the attractive stained-glass doors. The public bar is a very traditional room with a dark wood counter and walls lined with old brewery mirrors. A cosy little snug leads off at the back. Alongside Caledonian Deuchars IPA there are three regularly changing beers which can often include far-flung guests from south of the border although they are usually pale rather than dark.

Leaving Staggs be aware that it's a good walk, about two miles, before the next refreshment stop; but if you want to cut it short the useful No. 26 bus (destination Seton Sands) leaves from the main road, Bridge Street, on the other side of the Brunton Hall and calls both at the Levenhall Arms (on the big roundabout at the east end of town), and right outside the Prestoungrange Gothenburg at Prestonpans.

For those hardly souls who are walking, return down the North High Street to rejoin the river, cross by the footbridge and turn left to follow the riverside walk, which at the next bridge becomes The John Muir Way. The path follows the coastline from the river estuary here in Musselburgh, right the way around what once was a series of ash lagoons for the nearby Cockenzie power station but which are steadily being reclaimed and have important wildlife value. Indeed this is a stretch where you are very likely to find twitchers with their binoculars on both sides of the path. Coastal views here are excellent: from Edinburgh on one side right round to the big power station

joins the road by Adam Ferguson House, Eskmills and soon you pass the footbridge and then climb some steps to carefully cross the bypass road (the old route of the railway line) to rejoin the river before reaching the photogenic old stone bridge of Musselburgh. Here you cross the bridge and turn right onto the left bank of the river into the old town of Fisherrow, from which the main town grew up.

Now in Eskdale West, follow the river downstream to the road bridge. Keep to the riverside and walk under the bridge continuing along Eskdale West to Eskdale House – recognisable by the striking pineapple building. Turn left shortly into North High Street where soon you will meet the Brunton Theatre on your left and finally, immediately opposite, the **The Volunteer Arms** ⊤, better known as Staggs after the family whose pub this has been since 1858.

Levenhall Arms

chimneys close to the eastern horizon.

At a signboard for Levenhall Links, a path leaves to head inland. This is decision time because if you're walking to the Levenhall Arms, you need to head inland here (see below). My recommendation is to continue along the coast path for the final mile and a half to Prestonpans, and 'bag' the Levenhall Arms by bus on the way back to Edinburgh, in which case continue ahead until the path is pushed briefly away from the shore (as of early 2010) by the last active ash lagoon and swings left inland of this close to the coastal road where the route from the Levenhall Arms runs parallel to the road.

Otherwise head inland on the path past the bird reserve and the car park and continue up towards the race course following the (sometimes muddy) road round to the left. Aim for a (legal!) gap in the fence at the end of the race course and follow the grassy path towards some older houses and, via this lane, out right by the **Levenhall Arms 2**. This traditional pub right on the big roundabout retains its two room layout with a small third room used for darts, leading off the public bar. The well-kept beers are a regular, Stewart IPA, plus one or two guests depending upon the time of year -- and be warned that in winter the pub doesn't open until 2pm. The pub has recently started hosting its own beer festivals and judging by the success so far is set to continue this welcome

trend. Food is served all day until 8pm in the quieter lounge.

Continuing towards Prestonpans, turn left out the pub and along the road. At the end of the line of housing head through a gate across a green, and pick up a good path which you follow to the right. It is joined shortly by the main John Muir Way path from the coast, and then follows the main road at a safe distance past the Prestongrange Industrial Heritage museum (free admission, but only opens summer, see www.prestoungrange.org for details). It's probably better to visit by bus after leaving Prestonpans, if you are planning on visiting. The path makes a double dog-leg past an industrial site (look out for the cycle route signs), and now rejoins the sea wall, and over some dunes with good views of the power station ahead, until you reach the outskirts of Prestonpans.

The town, named after its salt pans, saw Bonnie Prince Charlie in action at the eponymous battle here in 1745, and developed its wealth through its soap and brewing industries in addition to salt and oysters. The path turns 90° inland for a short distance to join the road close to some murals, for which Prestonpans is well known. Now simply follow the road into town and the **Prestoungrange Gothenburg 3** is a five minute walk. Alternatively at low tide, you can follow the sea wall and then the beach to emerge via some steps right at the pub above some impressive murals and opposite the town's weird totem pole! In the car park opposite the pub, in addition to the totem pole, is a map of the Prestonpans

Mural under the Goth car park

left: **Prestoungrange Gothenburg** right: **House beer taps at the Prestoungrange Gothenburg**

murals trail. As mentioned earlier, there's one on the beach immediately below the sea wall here, which depicts local industries.

The Goth (nicknamed not after the weirdly dressed yoof cult but after the Swedish system of encouraging temperance and community benefit – see box) is quite simply one of Scotland's pub treasures. Built in 1908 in Arts and Crafts style it was empty for some time before the current owners beautifully restored it and reopened the pub in 2003, when it won a CAMRA award for the quality of the work. The spacious public bar is a tremendous example of Art Nouveau styling, with green tiles and white woodwork dominant. There's even a small jug bar (off sales servery) with some intricate carved woodwork. There's a panelled lounge next door and more modern rooms upstairs but the main bar is the place to admire this gem at its best.

The other great news is that one the on-site brewery has been reopened and is now producing three excellent cask beers, an IPA, 80/- and (unusually perhaps given the Scottish palate), a porter. There's a wide-ranging and award-winning menu catering for all diets. The pub has once more become a key part of the local community with a range of events including a monthly folk night; and it is a key sponsor of the local Arts Festival.

If you're here for a lengthy session you can relax, for although the railway station is some distance away on the edge of town, the very frequent 26 bus runs pretty late and is therefore the best plan for returning to Edinburgh. The stop is a few yards down the road (turn left out of the pub); but remember to make time to visit the Levenhall Arms if you missed it on the way out.

PUB INFORMATION

1 The Volunteer Arms (Staggs)
81 North High St, Musselburgh, EH21 6JE
0131 665 9654
www.staggsbar.com
Opening Hours: 11 (12.30 Sun)-11 (midnight Thu & Sun; 12.30am Fri & Sat)
CAMRA Regional Inventory

2 Levenhall Arms
10 Ravensheugh Rd, Musselburgh, EH21 7PP
0131 665 3220
Opening Hours: 12 (12.30 Sun)-11 (midnight Thu & Sun; 1am Fri & Sat; in winter opens at 2pm (1pm Fri & Sat)
CAMRA Regional Inventory

2 Prestoungrange Gothenburg
227-9 High St, Prestonpans, EH32 9BE
01875 819922
www.thegoth.co.uk
Opening Hours: 12-2.30, 5-11 Tue-Thu; 12-midnight Fri & Sat; 12.30-11 Sun; closed Mon
CAMRA National Inventory (Part 2)

Roll of Honour at Staggs including CAMRA National Pub of the Year certificate

Linlithgow Town Trail

WALK INFORMATION

Start/Finish: Linlithgow rail station

Access: Trains to Linlithgow

Distance: 1.2 miles (1.8 km)

Key attractions: Union Canal and Canal Wharf Museum, Annet House Museum, Linlithgow Palace and the Peel, Linlithgow Loch, St. Michael's Parish Church

The pubs: The Four Marys, Platform 3

Links: None

Steeped in history, Linlithgow has a royal pedigree difficult to match in all of Scotland. Its central location helped to make it an early royal residence, and by the beginning of the 12th century it was already well established as a burgh with a mansion and a church, given by King David to the newly founded Augustinian Priory of St Andrews. In 1349 the Black Death reached Scotland and killed a third of the population of Edinburgh, and the King, parliament and court took refuge in Linlithgow, which grew to outstrip even Stirling in importance. The once magnificent place was the birthplace of James V and Mary Queen of Scots, whilst it was important enough for Cromwell to install himself here after defeating the Scots at Dunbar in 1650. Today it's more of a backwater, but the ruined palace in its splendid loch-side setting is a focal point to a short but varied walk taking in two contrasting but top-notch pubs where you can expect well-kept and varied ales.

Gateway crests to Linlithgow Palace

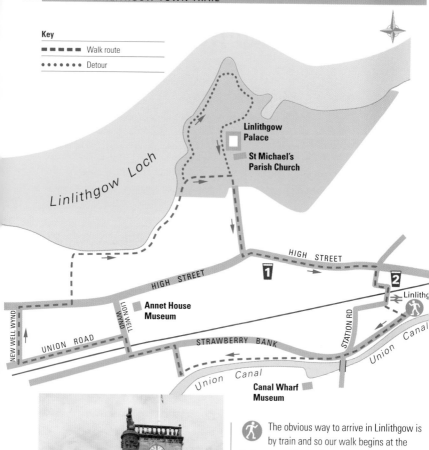

Key

▬ ▬ ▬ ▬ ▬ Walk route

● ● ● ● ● ● Detour

Linlithgow Loch

Linlithgow Palace

St Michael's Parish Church

HIGH STREET

1

2

Linlith[

Annet House Museum

NEW WELL WYND

LION WELL WYND

UNION ROAD

STRAWBERRY BANK

STATION RD

Union Canal

Union Canal

Canal Wharf Museum

Cross Well and Town House

The obvious way to arrive in Linlithgow is by train and so our walk begins at the station, one of the best preserved of the old Edinburgh and Glasgow Railway Company. Leave the platform via the car park into Back Station Road, turn right and, forking left after 200 yards continue uphill to join the canal at the bridge. Here is the restored Linlithgow basin of the Union Canal (see box). It's a charming spot especially in sunshine; and if you cross the bridge and walk down to the wharf (in summer when they're open) you can visit the canal museum and tea room (once a stables) and even, at weekends, take a boat trip organised by the Canal Society. To continue you need to re-cross the canal and follow the towpath on the northern side past the Learmonth Gardens in which you should be able to spot the impressive Ross Doocot (dovecot or pigeonhouse), dating back to the 16th century with nearly 400 nest boxes. A little further along on the opposite side of the canal is Rosemount

Palace and St. Michael's Church from the canal towpath

Just before the next bridge leave the canal and head downhill to the right past the former Ebenezer Chapel (a plaque in the gable end recalls the use of the building as a meeting house of the local Evangelical Union). Turn left into Royal Terrace, a fine street of 19th century stone houses, and cross the railway by the footbridge, turning left into Union Road. A short distance along the road dips down towards a cross roads, but before the foot of the brae turn right by the chapel into New Well Wynd, a little lane which leads in no more than a hundred yards to the main road. A little west (left) of this point stood the old West Port, the western gateway to the town. The pubs hereabouts are said to have been established to cater for travel-

Park inside which is the fountainhead of the Cross Well, a prominent feature of the town centre we'll encounter later on the walk.

THE UNION CANAL

The Union Canal opened in 1822 and was known as the Edinburgh and Glasgow Union Canal. Among other things it was intended to ensure the easy transport of coal into the capital from the big coalfields around Glasgow.

It followed the contours of the landscape, so there are no locks along its length. The cost was boosted however by the need to build three large aqueducts, among them the Slateford aqueduct just outside Edinburgh (see walk 16) and another just west of Linlithgow at Muiravonside, which at 810ft long and 86ft high is the second longest in Britain.

Although the canal was built without locks, a way needed to be found of linking the Union Canal with the Forth and Clyde Canal where they met near Falkirk, a difference of 110ft. The answer was a staircase of 11 locks over a half mile length of canal.

Like many canals however its life was short because the railways undermined its profitability, and for many years it ran at a loss. This ended in 1965 with the formal closure of the canal by Act of Parliament. The canal bed was severed in one place by a motorway, in another by a new housing estate, and the lock staircase was removed.

The restoration of the Forth & Clyde and Union Canals came after a groundswell of support for canal restoration – and the Millennium Link, as the £85m restoration of the two canals was known, became a reality after much hard work. In this project pride of place must go to one of the modern wonders of the British canal system, the Falkirk Wheel, an ingenious contraption used to link the two canals. This was opened by the Queen in May 2002. You can find out more about the Falkirk Wheel at www.thefalkirkwheel.co.uk

Union Canal wharf

lers shut out for the night! The tall spire to your left is of St. Ninian's church, but we turn right and head back into the town centre. Look out immediately for the stone well head of New Well, one of many former well heads, before crossing by the lights just a few yards along. Now take the first left into Water Yett. Although we are turning off here the main street has a couple of noteworthy sights if you want to detour a short way: further along on the right tucked in just behind some tenements is St. Peter's Episcopal Church, an interesting interwar Byzantine style building, and shortly beyond that is Annet House, an 18th century merchant's house which is now home to the Linlithgow museum.

Water Yett leads down to the shore of Linlithgow Loch offering you a commanding view of the old Palace to your left, sitting high up on a promontory above the water. The loch itself is a remnant of the last ice age when a large lump of ice left by a retreating glacier was surrounded by sediment and subsequently melted. Head round the loch towards the palace, ideally taking the obvious sloping path through the gateway which doubles back fairly gently to the grassy open space around the ruins. Alternatively continue along the shore path a bit further and climb up the grass on a gentler gradient from the other side. The parkland here is known as the

Peel, after the wooden palisade, or pele, which once protected the fort. I cannot do justice to Linlithgow Palace here but the present building dates back to the early 15th century although it took some two centuries to complete. James V was born here as was Mary, Queen of Scots. The palace was fortified and occupied by Oliver Cromwell in the 1650s, but was gutted by fire in 1746 after the Duke of Cumberland's soldiers occupied it and it has been roofless ever since. It is still impressive though, not least the magnificent Great Hall. The Palace is cared for by Historic Scotland, and there is an admission charge to go inside. If the weather is fine the Peel is a great place to rest before heading off. From the top of the peel look out for a couple of small islands in the loch over to the east (right). These are man-made islands which once contained crannogs – wooden roundhouses which were once a common form of settlement in Scotland and Ireland, some built as early as 5000 years ago. Beyond the loch there are good views towards the steep wooded slopes of Airngath Hill, below which the M9 runs (almost apologetically by the brash standards of motorways) through the trees.

Heading down to the Palace gateway, although it will have caught your eye long before, is the very handsome church of St. Michael, one of Scotland's best parish churches. It was consecrated in 1242, but following a fire was rebuilt in much its present form in the mid fifteenth century. In 1821, the tower lost its 15th-century stone crown – to be replaced in 1964 by today's distinctive and striking aluminium spire. Noteworthy interior features include the pulpit, stained glass and the burgh war memorial.

Pass through the Palace gateway into Kirkgate, but turn around immediately to view the set of four carved panels above, representing the orders of knighthood of James V: the Golden Fleece, St. Michael, the Thistle and the Garter. Note too, as you

The Palace and St. Michael's Church sit on a prominent site above the loch

walk downhill, the series of plaques recording the royal line of succession from Mary, Queen of Scots to the present day.

You now reach the centre of Linlithgow by the Cross, one of Scotland's best civic spaces, although rather the poorer for the brash modern flats on your right. Known as the Vennel, these were put up in 1967 and remain even to this day a source of controversy since several fine old houses were destroyed to build them. They certainly sit rather uncomfortably with their neighbors, the Tudor style (but Victorian) Sheriff Courthouse and the neo Georgian interwar county buildings just beyond.

You're probably ready for a drink by now though after all this sightseeing, so let's leave the rest of the sights around the cross until later. Head across the High Street and slightly to your left to the **Four Marys** **1** . The unusual name of the pub comes from the four ladies-in-waiting of Mary Queen of Scots who as we have noted was born at the palace nearby. The building is an old one, perhaps dating back to the 16th century and has been a domestic house and, interestingly, a chemist shop run by the Waldie family – it was David Waldie who recognised

the aneaesthetic properties of chloroform, and a plaque outside commemorates him. In fact the Four Marys has only been a pub since the late 1970's and is now owned by the Belhaven brewery although wisely they also offer an impressive range of four changing guest beers in addition to their own perfectly acceptable ales and Deuchars IPA, served from an array of no less than eight hand pumps which dominate the carpeted front bar of this spacious 'L' shaped pub. You can expect your beer to be in fine form here too, for this, Linlithgow's premier real ale outlet, was the regional CAMRA branch pub of the year in 2009, and went on to be joint runner-up in the national competition. As if there weren't enough ales to choose from, there is a Beer Festival twice a year, at the ends of May and October. Food from an extensive menu is available daily until 9pm in the bar, or in the spacious and formal dining room towards the rear of the pub.

Finally, there's a beer garden at the rear if the weather permits…

Back in the Cross, the spacious town square outside the Four Marys, don't miss (as if you could) the elaborate Cross Well, a replica of an earlier original destroyed by Cromwell. This

An impressive range of handpumps at the Four Marys bar

one, dating from 1807, was made by one Robert Gray, a one-handed Edinburgh stonemason. It's overlooked by the impressive Town House, (or Burgh Halls) with its impressive external staircase built in 1668-70 to replace the original tolbooth, also demolished on the orders of Oliver Cromwell. Now in use partly as a Community Arts facility, it's currently (2010) being restored and enlarged at the rear but without altering its well loved frontage onto the Cross itself.

An array of *Good Beer Guides* at the Four Marys

Continue, when you're ready, east along the High Street past the Victoria Hall, once a cinema and then an amusement arcade. Just before our next refreshment stop note the attractive buildings of Hamilton's Land, with their crow-stepped gables – they were restored by the National Trust in 1958. Opposite, on the right hand side is the well head of St. Michael's Well, topped by a winged figure and the town's coat of arms: the

back bitch, tied to a tree on an island. Anyway, enough culture for the moment – we're now close by our last port of call, just before the roundabout at the end of the High Street, on the corner of Station Approach, is **Platform 3** 2. This little howff was once the public bar of the adjacent hotel but became a pub in its own right in 1998 and comes complete with its own little train set high above the punters on the wall. Expect a lively community local with a band of regulars propping up the bar; and well-kept ales. Caledonian Deuchars IPA is the regular here, but the second handpump plays host to a changing range of guests, usually from the Stewart or Cairngorm breweries. Snacks are available at lunchtimes. Even if you have a good session in here you'd be hard pressed to miss the lane uphill to the station right outside the door – but don't miss the last train…

PUB INFORMATION

1 **Four Marys**
65-67 High St, Linlithgow, EH49 7ED
01506 842171
www.thefourmarys.co.uk
Opening Hours: 12 (12.30 Sun)-11 (midnight Thu-Sat)

2 **Platform 3**
1a High St, Linlithgow, EH49 7AB
01506 847405
www.platform3.co.uk
Opening Hours: 10.30 (12.30 Sun)-midnight (1am Fri & Sat)

Adam Smith's 'Lang Toun' – A Kirkcaldy Town Walk

WALK INFORMATION

Start: Kirkcaldy rail station

Finish: Feuars Arms

Access: Trains to Kircaldy

Distance: 2.3 miles (3.6km)

Key attractions: Kirkcaldy old kirk, Merchant's house, Dysart conservation village (2 miles), Ravenscraig castle, Kirkcaldy museum and art gallery, Easter Links fair (see www.linksmarket.co.uk for details)

The pubs: Robert Nairn, Harbour Bar, Feuars Arms

Links: None

The 'Lang Toun' – so called because of its mile-long main street – is industrially a shadow of its former self. Nobody arriving today would recognise the oft quoted lines from MC Smith's poem 'The Boy in the Train': "For I ken mysel' by the queer-like smell/That the next stop's Kirkcaddy!" He was referring to the distinctive aroma of the linoleum factories which came to epitomise this important town, the largest in Fife. Today most of the lino factories are gone and the harbour is full of apartments rather than ships; but it's still worth making the trip across the Forth Bridge. The town has a wealth of historical associations, for example Adam Smith and Gordon Brown were both brought up here; and there are good buildings, old and new, If you're only here for the beer, our pubs offer a wide selection of ales and in the Feuars Arms you'll see one of the best examples of ceramic work in a Scottish pub, not to mention some urinary excellence that few British boozers can approach!

The handsome facade of Betty Nicols bar

The fastest trains take a little over half an hour from Edinburgh, and arrive at the ultra modern station – rebuilt in 1989 after a fire destroyed its predecessor – on the outskirts of the town centre. Cross under the subway and leave the station on the southern side, emerging immediately into a public garden in front of the imposing museum and library. This was built

thanks to the generosity of John Nairn, one of the family of linoleum manufacturers, and was opened in 1925. Walk diagonally across the garden towards the traffic roundabout keeping as a beacon the slender green clock tower of the Town House ahead of you. Cross the street and head down Wemyssfield towards the Town House. This impressive listed civic building was begun in 1939 but not completed until 1956. Turning left from Wemyssfield into Hunter Street with the rear end of Tesco to guide you, you'll pass Hunter House, formerly a hospital for the poor, but built originally in 1795 as St. Brycedale House and probably designed by Robert Adam. The two side wings are modern additions.

At the end of the street is the Kirk, or the Old Parish Church, which has been retired from active service but is set in an attractive churchyard and worth a brief detour. The tower is medieval and dates from about 1500 but the rest of the building is early 19th century. The group of buildings on Kirk Wynd as we turn downhill by the old church is one of the most attractive remaining in

Tiled picture in the Feuars Arms

Key

▬ ▬ ▬ ▬ ▬ Walk route

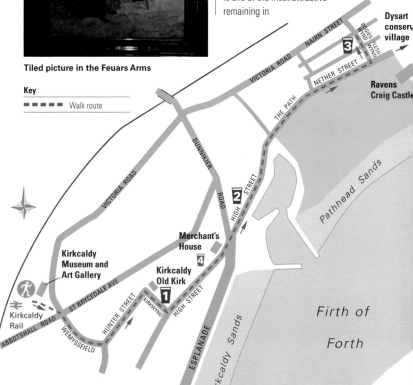

Kirkcaldy. It includes Hendry Hall, the baronial style building immediately under the church. By now you'll probably be ready for your first refreshment stop, and help is at hand, for a little further down the street is the **Robert Nairn 1**. Part of J D Wetherspoon's Lloyd's No. 1 empire, the pub, occupying a former bank premises, remains true to the JDW tradition of promoting local names and

Adam Smith plaque

places, in this case the oldest son of the linoleum magnate Michael (although it's not obvious why they didn't honour the great man himself). It's very much the usual Wetherspoon format but you can expect the beers to be in good condition and the choice to be a good one. Walk down to the High Street at the bottom of the hill, looking out for the plaque on the wall (at No. 220) by the bakers commemorating Adam Smith. It was in a house on this side that Smith who was born

in the town lived with his mother while he wrote his famous treatise 'The Wealth of Nations'. Turn left down the High Street and in a few minutes you'll pass the **Betty Nicols Bar 4**.

A listed building built in the late 18th century, the bar is located on the ground floor of a stone four-storey tenement. The frontage of the property is very attractive with red granite facings and a coloured stained glass window depicting a ship in a roundel, a link with Kirkcaldy's maritime heritage. Inside, the public bar retains its original dado height ceramic tiles, a good back gantry with a decorative cornice and ceiling above. Cask ale availability seems to be a wee bit patchy so if you do venture inside for a drink be prepared for the worst! A short distance beyond Betty Nicols the High Street joins the Esplanade,

The grade 'A' listed Merchant's House

and here on the left, partly occupied by the town's tourist office, is the Merchant's House. This is an outstanding old building, grade 'A' listed, and just the place to work up a thirst for the next pub stop just beyond. To appreciate the frontage you

Coat of arms in old Kirkcaldy

have to stand back from it, perhaps over on the Esplanade. The house dates back to just after the Reformation, in 1590, when it was built by the Law family. Internally one of its treasures is a fine mural painting of a merchant ship, thought to be the Angel, which conveyed Anne of Denmark to Scotland after marrying King James VI. When the tourist office is open you can pass through the pend to the back courtyard and admire the rear of the building which, more than the frontage, conveys a real sense of antiquity. There are some old ovens set into a wall, for the place was once used as a bakery. You can also climb up to the remarkable steeply rising rigg garden at the rear of the property. A rigg is the long narrow plot fronting onto the main street which was the normal unit of ownership in the Scottish medieval and early modern town. The rigg could be divided into foreland, inner land and back land, with the main buildings on or near the frontage, and workshops and gardens behind. The word probably derives

from rig (ridge) as used for the long narrow strips into which open fields were divided, and the open field system before the enclosures and clearances was known in Scotland as Runrig.

Take care crossing the wide street here, probably best to cross to the Esplanade side before the road junction since we want to stay on the lower road here, closest to the shore, as we continue eastwards. Before feeling disappointed at the rather bleak esplanade behind you, remember that Kirkcaldy was not built for beauty and the tourists but for industry! On the right is the old harbour, frankly looking pretty sorry for itself with some uninspiring modern apartments lining the waterside; much more attractive is the white house with the gable across the street. This is Sailor's Walk, even older than the Merchant's House (parts date back to around 1460). It has been restored, and exhibits some typical traditional Scottish architectural touches, including the crow stepped gables and the deep set gable windows. Harbour House, an attractive 18th century stone building, sits behind the street frontage hereabouts – a reminder of the days when Kirkcaldy had a significant maritime trade.

Anyway time for a drink – a few yards beyond is Kirkcaldy's best real ale emporium, the **Harbour Bar 2**. Despite the demise of the harbour after which it is named, the eponymous bar is going strong and regularly wins the local CAMRA branch's Pub of the Year accolade. With a micro-brewery behind the pub, and a guest beer list which is ambitious and forever changing this pub runs the nearest thing to a permanent beer festival from its six handpumps. You can expect the welcome to be warm and the ale to be in very good nick! Moreover the interior is a traditional and unspoilt

Kirkcaldy – roofs, turrets and gables

Hunter House

one with some inter-war work on the off-sales hatch in front of you on entry, and the retention of the two bar layout. Watch out for the afternoon closure early in the week.

Leaving the Harbour, continue along the main road which leads uphill towards the district of Pathhead. This was once the main industrial area of town, and as you cross the East Burn some of the old mill buildings survive – the handsome one close by is the office to Hutchison's flour millers, who still operate the flour silos along the shore. Note the lovely fan glass window above the door, and a horse gin outside, once used for threshing grain. At the top of the hill is Path House, a late 17th century building, and right opposite a road leads down to a car park which gives access to the ruins of Ravenscraig Castle. On this site, which is now parkland, stood the original Nairn linoleum factory.

The castle, one of the first to be built for defence with guns, was commissioned by James II in 1460. It occupies a commanding site overlooking the Firth of Forth, and was yet another place visited by Cromwell on his extensive tour of destruction/liberation. Access is limited but it's worth the detour down from the main road to wander round, not least to make room for a pint in your next and last port of call. Either way, walk along to or make your way back up to the junction, turning inland at the near (Kirkcaldy) end of the

three housing tower blocks, and head into an area of modern housing. You'll be able to see the **Feuars Arms** 🖪 as it's only a short walk up. The name refers to holder of a tenancy, the duty of which was paid either in money or in kind, usually in grain. Having just come from a pub of beer superlatives, now you've arrived at one where the

The Harbour Bar

left: **Tiled bar counter at the Feuars Arms** right: **Stained glass at the Feuars Arms**

pub fittings and especially the display of ceramics are among the best in Scotland. The Art Nouveau style, evident for example along the 60' bar counter completely fronted in brown tiles, comes from the 1902 remodelling of this late Victorian building. From the mosaic floor to the solid mahogany gantry with its little office complete with clock; and the superb stained and etched glass the whole place is a real treasure – and it doesn't end in the bar, for the gents' (women have to ask, and pick their time carefully!) is a temple of excellence with its possibly unique glass-panelled Doulton cistern above a pair of marble-framed urinals, tiled walls and a mosaic floor.

All of this of course, you have drunk in whilst enjoying a pint: here the policy is one ale on sale at a time, and the choice is a rotation from one of three breweries: Brewdog, Inveralmond and Deeside. Lunches are served, along with evening meals at weekends; but I recommend phoning ahead to check if you're intending to eat here.

Several buses drop back into town from the main road above the castle if you don't want to walk back – or if you're in a group heading back to the station a cab may be a good option. If you have time to spare, Dysart, one of Fife's many interesting old coastal villages, is another mile or so along the coast here.

PUB INFORMATION

1 Robert Nairn
2/6 Kirk Wynd, Kirkcaldy, KY1 1EH
01592 205049
www.jdwetherspoon.co.uk/
home/pubs/the-robert-nairn
Opening Hours: 11 (12.30
Sun)-midnight

2 Harbour Bar
473 High St, Kirkcaldy, KY1 2SN
01592 264270
www.fyfebrewery.co.uk
Opening Hours: 11-3, 5-midnight; 11-midnight Thu-Sat; 12.30-midnight Sun
CAMRA Regional Inventory

2 Feuars Arms
28 Bogies Wynd, Kirkcaldy, KY1 2PH
01592 205 577
www.thefeuarsarms.co.uk
Opening Hours: 11.30 (12 Sat,
12.30 Sun)-midnight
*CAMRA National Inventory
(Part 2)*

TRY ALSO:

4 Betty Nichols Bar
297 High St, Kirkcaldy, KY1 1JL
01592 642 083
www.bettynicols.co.uk
Opening Hours: 11 (12.30
Sun)-10 (11 Wed & Thu;
midnight Fri & Sat)

Cistern at the Feuars Arms

Georgian Haddington

WALK INFORMATION

Start/Finish: Town centre, adjacent Town House

Access: Buses – ideally the fast X6/X8 Services (First Group) from St. Andrew Square

Distance: 1.3 miles (2km)

Key attractions: Haddington House and Pleasance garden, Nungate Bridge, St. Mary's Church, Poldrate Mill, Glenkinchie distillery – Pencaitland (5 miles)

The pubs: Waterloo Bistro, Tyneside Tavern, Victoria Inn

Links: to walk 24

See www.scotland.org.uk/guide/Haddington

There can be few more attractive towns for their size than Haddington, with nearly 300 listed buildings, many dating back to the 18th century. In a strategic location surrounded by some of the country's most productive land the town was granted a royal charter as long ago as the 12th century, and was connected to the then-busy seaport of Aberlady to the north. In the fifteenth century Haddington was the fourth largest town in Scotland, and a century later in the days of Henry VIII the Scottish Parliament met here. The walk takes in most of the best sights in this compact town, as well as incorporating a pleasant riverside stroll. Beer choice is adequate but enthusiastic beerhounds may consider combining this route with the Dunbar route (walk 24) which is another half an hour on the same bus from Edinburgh.

The best way of getting here is by the fast X6/X8 services (First Group) from St. Andrew Square, the journey taking about 45 minutes. Get off the bus at the junction of the High Street and Market Street by the Town House – with its prominent steeple it's difficult to miss.

The Town House was originally built in 1748 but the steeple is 19th century. It dominates the town, for although the church is large, it is tucked away

The Tyneside Tavern stands next to the old mill

Haddington High Street and the Town House

down by the river and has a squat tower rather than a soaring steeple! If you enjoy good buildings the whole town is a treat: Court Street, behind you, is wide and stately, in contrast with the earlier, and narrower, pattern of streets along

and between Market and High Streets, which fork either side of the Town House. Take the right fork and walk down the High Street passing a little Mercat Cross, down to the curious

George Hotel with its castellated folly partially closing off the end of the street. Cross straight over into Church Street.

Now a bit of a backwater, Church Street and its continuation The Sands was in ancient times the main route leading down to the river crossing at the Nungate Bridge. There are several interesting buildings all the way down. Past Peter Potter Gallery there is reputedly the oldest bowling green in Scotland, whilst opposite is another impressive doocot (dovecote) that now houses the community tourist information office in season. The bridge is now pedestrianised but lays claim to being the oldest remaining in Scotland. It's where the French gathered in 1549 to assist the Scottish against the English who were occupying Haddington. Hangings took place under its western arch.

Across the river on Gifford Gate is the birthplace, as legend has it, of John Knox the famous religious reformer. Should you wish to see this then cross the bridge and keep right upstream. Pass the houses on the left then look out for an oak tree and black metal railings and a gate that leads up steps to the memorial stone.

Back on the bank closest to the town, pick up the river path at the bridge – the scene here is dominated by the huge bulk of St. Mary's Church, the largest parish church in Scotland. The Gothic building dates back to the 14th century although it took a hundred years to complete. It lay partially in ruins for over 400 years before its restoration in 1971. The church is open to visitors May – September from 1.30 to 4pm daily.

The river path crosses the narrow tail race of the Poldrate Mill close to the rear of the church. Follow this with the river on your left, until you reach the road and the Waterloo Bridge. Across the road to the right is the Poldrate mill, no longer used for its original purpose but now a community centre specialising in youth work and arts and crafts. Immediately to its left is the first of your refreshment stops, the **Waterloo Bistro** 🛈, housed in an attractive collection of buildings with a distinctly continental feel. Enter via the courtyard, with the bar left and the bistro right. This is an upmarket venue specialising in food and wine – but it does offer hand pulled Caledonian Deuchars IPA, and

The courtyard at the Waterloo Bistro

The Nungate Bridge

left: **Tyneside Tavern interior** right: **The Victoria Inn**

whether inside or outside in the courtyard, a very convivial environment in which to drink it. You can still get a drink in the bistro even if the bar is closed.

On leaving, squeeze through the alleyway by the mill and you immediately come upon the next port of call, the **Tyneside Tavern** 2 . Housed in a pair of stone houses with gables fronting the street, this is a more traditional bar, with the public bar to the left and the lounge bar to the right. The five handpulls dispense Caledonian Deuchars IPA and 80, together with three rotating guest beers. Hearty good value meals using local ingredients are served in both bars luchtimes and evenings.

To see Haddington House – the oldest dwelling in town, but now offices – and visit its distinctive period garden The Pleasance, then turn left out the Tyneside Tavern, past the gates of St. Mary's Church and it's a short distance up on the right.

Return to the river path and continue along the river for about 600 yards until you get to the weir. Disregard the first path off to the right, and instead cross the small bridge over the mill race and walk straight ahead at 90° away from the river and shortly join a narrow road. This has playing fields on both sides and then

a right (at the T junction) and left dog-leg, brings you to the main road. Here, turn right and walk down to the junction with Station Road and Court Street by the statue of Ferguson of Raith, a former MP for the burgh of Haddington.

Turn right into Court Street, a splendid avenue with buildings of note everywhere, particularly at the far end on the right, where the council buildings and Corn Exchange lie close together. Just beyond, prominently on the corner just before the Town House and steeple where we started our walk, is the **Victoria Inn** 3 . This is another upmarket venue with a well-regarded menu. Despite external appearances the bar area is actually quite small, and arranged around a horseshoe bar counter. There are two regularly changing beers available on tap, and it's a great place to watch the Haddington world go by while you wait for your bus back to Edinburgh. The stop is back on the High Street near the Mercat Cross.

▶ LINK ◀

PUB INFORMATION

1 **Waterloo Bistro**
Tyne House, Poldrate,
Haddington, EH41 4DA
01620 822 100
www.waterloobistro.co.uk
Opening Hours: 12-late

2 **Tyneside Tavern**
10 Poldrate, Haddington,
EH41 4DA
01620 822221
www.tynesidetavern.com
Opening Hours: 11-11 (midnight
Thu; 1am Fri & Sat); 12.30-midnight Sun

3 **Victoria Inn**
9 Court St, Haddington,
EH41 3JD
01620 823 332
www.theavenuerestaurant.co.uk
Opening Hours: 11 (12.30 Sun)-
11 (midnight Thu-Sat)

▶ LINK ◀ Walk 24 **A Dunbar Coastal Trail** (page 129) from Haddington you can get the bus to Belhaven and Dunbar, but both routes together would make a long day, so best tackled in summer by energetic walkers/ drinkers!

North Berwick to Gullane – Edinburgh's Golf Coast

WALK INFORMATION

Start: North Berwick rail station

Access: Train to North Berwick; Buses X5 from St. Andrew Square calling at Gullane, Dirleton and North Berwick. Service 124 also connects the three villages for local travel

Distance: North Berwick Circuit 3 miles (4.9km); Gullane to Dirleton 5.3 miles (8.6km); link section 1.5 miles (2.4km)

Key attractions: The Scottish Sea Bird Centre www.seabird.org, North Berwick Law, Gullane golf courses, John Muir Way, Dirleton Castle www. historic-scotland.gov.uk

The pubs: Auld Hoose, Ship Inn, Nether Abbey Hotel, Old Clubhouse, Castle Inn

Links: None

Easily and quickly accessible from Edinburgh by train or bus, the North Sea coast around North Berwick (not to be confused with Berwick-upon-Tweed which is much further off) offers the drinking walker a flexible range of possibilities from a simple town circuit to a much longer coastal ramble best left to the fitter and more experienced hiker. Good local bus services and a couple of simple inland paths offer links between the coastal settlements so that each of the pubs here is accessible to all and a full day's beerhunting can be put together. It's worth studying the map and route directions carefully before deciding what to tackle. You'll certainly enjoy the coast path a lot more on a warm sunny day; and if the tide is at least partially out, things are easier.

The Auld Hoose

You have a few options on this route so you can adapt it to fit the time of year, your interests and fitness level. The short walk around North Berwick offers an interesting look around an award-winning town with optional detours to the Scottish seabird centre or up the distinctive North Berwick Law. Combine this with a bus trip to Dirleton and/ or Gullane for a full day's beer-hunting.

Craigleith island viewed across the golf links at North Berwick

Sea views from North Berwick Law, an optional climb for the energetic

Alternatively take the bus from North Berwick station (or the bus direct from Edinburgh – the X5 does the trip from St. Andrew Square in 50 minutes) to Gullane to start the long walk to Dirleton. You could then take another bus from the Castle Inn at Dirleton to North Berwick, or bypass Dirleton to walk the link route back to North Berwick.

Keep an eye on the tides if you're tackling the longer route – they can work to your advantage, but can also catch unwary walkers off-guard. For online tide tables go to www.bbc. co.uk/weather/coast/tides click on Scotland, then Dunbar or Fidra. At lower tides it's an attractive option to walk along the shore to North Berwick without heading inland following the John Muir way as in the text below – remember there is a broad right of access in Scotland and this allows you to cross golf courses as long as you don't interfere with the game!

Town circuit – North Berwick

North Berwick is an attractive town which has won the prestigious Rosebowl Trophy for Scotland's most beautiful town in 2007 and 2009; there are a couple of lively web sites with information about the area www.northberwick.org.uk and www.north-berwick.co.uk.

Exit the station into the car park, and look for the path dropping down across the street close to the pedestrian crossing – this leads down to Abbey Road, which merges into the western end of the High Street. Follow the main street east down to the town centre. A good place to aim for first of all, particularly if it's too early to start looking for a beer when you arrive, is the Scottish Seabird Centre in the Harbour. You can't really get lost in North Berwick but turn left at the end of the High Street and head right down Victoria Street to the sea. There's a fairly high admission charge if you actually want to go into the seabird centre; but boat trips for the Bass Rock, which is about three miles offshore to the east, also leave from here.

The Old Clubhouse, Gullane

There are two selected pubs in the town centre on our route – you could leave them until after the walk, and head back into town after the circuit; or tackle them now. You will have already passed close to the **Auld Hoose** 🔳 on Forth Street, the road running parallel to the High Street on the seaward side. It's a substantial, traditional stone building with a fairly unspoilt although partially opened out interior. The three bay gantry has carved pillars and supports several old whisky casks. The cask ale range however is often limited to Greene King Abbot Ale, which is quite a high gravity beer. Leaving the Auld Hoose and turning right and shortly right again you come

NORTH BERWICK LAW

Although definitely 'off piste' for the pub walks, more energetic drinkers may enjoy the ascent of this distinctive conical hill which rises behind the town, to a height of 615'. It's been a distant part of the background scenery on several walks in this book. Like the Bass Rock and Castle Rock in Edinburgh, North Berwick Law is an igneous volcanic plug, the remains of a vent in the volcano, subsequently eroded and smoothed by ice. There are, as you'd expect, panoramic views, from Edinburgh Castle and the Forth Bridge in the west across the Firth of Forth and Fife, around to Tantallon Castle in the east, and finally the Lammermuir Hills to the south. If you do make it to the summit you'll be able to inspect the replica fibreglass whale jawbone (!) forming a distinctive arch. The original collapsed in 2005, a victim of exposure to the elements.

into Quality Street. At the far end lies the **Ship Inn** 🔳. This is another traditional stone bar but inside the layout is open plan although there are several separate drinking areas. The pine floorboards are set off by a mahogany bar counter and a dark stained gantry. The Ship normally offers three cask ales, Caledonian Deuchars IPA and two guests. Lunches are available.

To pick up the walk route, go back to Forth Street and re-trace your steps until you reach the grassy esplanade. Or at low tide you could try your luck on the shore from the harbour... With the offshore island of Craigleith as your close companion you can simply walk around the seaward

NORTH BERWICK

Key

▬ ▬ ▬ ▬ Long walk

▬ ▬ ▬ ▬ Short walk

• • • • • • Link route

Bass Rock, an ancient volcanic plug, is a renowned seabird colony

Ship Inn

side of the golf links for the best part of half a mile until you reach a wall striking inland. Turn left here and follow the path across the golf course, taking care if golfers are around. The path will bring you out onto Hamilton Road with the Marine Hotel and modern flats on your left. Follow Hamilton Road through a quiet residential area to the main road. Turn left here and look out for the **Nether Abbey Hotel** 3 on your left. This recently refurbished hotel is the premier real ale destination in town: unless you're planning to overnight here head to the Fly Half Bar at the right hand end of the building. It's a bright open plan bar with the lower, L-shaped area given over for the drinkers. Don't be deceived by the chrome lager-style founts – the real ales are really real and dispensed in good condition, evidenced by the Abbey's lengthy run in successive editions of the *Good Beer Guide*. Expect Caledonian Deuchars IPA, Taylor Landlord, and up to two other rotating guest beers. As you'd expect in the hotel

you will be able to get something to eat here lunchtimes and evenings; and throughout the day Friday to Sunday.

To return to town, simply continue on the main road and straight ahead at the traffic lights. To return to the station, take the first right on the way to town (Ware Road) and just before the railway bridge, a footpath bears left to the platform, about six minutes walk from the hotel.

Coast walk – Gullane to Dirleton

Advice: This is a long walk, certainly not a pub to pub stroll. The coast path is not well signed, and in places is narrow with short steep sections. It's possible at lower states of the tide to skirt the more awkward bits by taking to the shore. Experienced and confident walkers will find no real difficulties but couch potatoes are advised that the inland route following the John Muir Way (see below; or the bus!) are simpler alternatives between Gullane and the Castle Inn at Dirleton.

Gullane, with its attractive sandy beach – one of the best in the Lothians – and characterful villas overlooking the bay, is synonymous with golf. Aside from the three courses of the Gullane Golf Club there's the world famous Muirfield course on the north east of the village. Altogether there are ten courses within a five mile radius.

Chances are you'll arrive in Gullane by bus. Ask for East Links Road, close to the church and library at the far (western) end of the main street. My recommendation, if you have time, would be to do the walk to Dirleton

You're never far from a golf course along this part of the Lothian coast

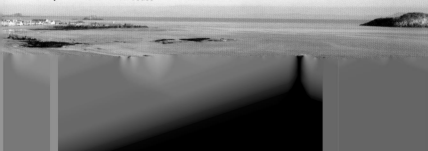

first, returning to Gullane by bus after visiting the Castle Inn. To reach the cask ale in Gullane, make directly for East Links road, by the green on the south side of the main street. As the road bends left, the **Old Clubhouse 4** occupies an enviable site with views over one of Gullane's numerous golf courses. There's an upmarket, comfortable and spacious lounge with dining area beyond. Beers are Caledonian Deuchars IPA, Timothy Taylor Landlord, and a guest.

To tackle the walk we need to find the sea! From the crossroads where East Links Road joins Main Street, directly across and straight ahead you'll see another green, called 'Goose Green' for some reason. Walk down and cross the green to the far opposite (north east) corner and into Marine Road from which point you'll see the sea. The road soon turns left but you want to join the grassy path and follow it to the shore, the eastern end of a sweeping sandy bay. Here we turn east (right) and head along the dunes below the famous Muirfield golf course. The route then skirts the edge of a plantation, just beyond which are the remains of a ruined cottage at the headland – the Black Rocks. Keep close to the across the sandy bay of Fresh Water Haven, beyond which is a wide area of sand dunes. There's a rather confusing network of paths here; the trick is to keep fairly close to the shore and if you feel you're going astray simply bear left until you pick up the coastline once again. As you round the next headland the path is now on the top of some low cliffs with an area of woodland ahead, although there have been recent clearances of scrub and vegetation. If the tide is in you'll need to keep to the clifftop path throughout this next section although at low tide it's an option with care to walk along the foreshore as an alternative. Some sections of the path here are narrow and steep, and at high tide the foreshore is not accessible.

Pass the prominent house on the seaward side, after which the path becomes rath-

DIRLETON

The conservation village of Dirleton, now happily by-passed by the main road, is arranged around a large green, with an historic church and the castle ruins in close attendance. The picturesque cottages around the village green in their pleasant setting have led some to call it the prettiest village in Scotland. The present parish church, built in the early years of the seventeenth century to replace the 12th century church of St. Andrew in Gullane, has been extended more than once, as is apparent from the interesting architecture. The curious neo-classical aisle projecting from the nave is thought to be one the earliest of its style in the country, while in 1836 the tower acquired its striking Gothic pinnacles.

Dirleton Castle was the 12th century stronghold of the De Vaux family, and is arguably the most imposing among several ruined castles in East Lothian, sitting as it does high up on a rocky knoll. It's well known for its beautiful gardens incorporating, according to the Guinness Book of Records, the world's longest herbaceous border. There's also an impressively situated bowling green. If you have time the castle is worth a visit, but there is an admission charge (currently £4.70).

er easier to navigate once again, with a plantation on your right and a sandy bay. The island offshore is Fidra, which is claimed as the inspiration for Robert Louis Stevenson's *Treasure Island*, with 'Spy-glass Hill' based on Yellowcraig on the mainland ahead. Stevenson certainly visited the island

The Old Clubhouse, Gullane

several times to witness the construction of the lighthouse, built by his grandfather's engineering company in 1885. The smaller island further east, Lamb Island, which comes into view as you round the headland, is potentially more significant than it looks: it was recently bought by spoon-bender Uri Geller who is apparently convinced that the juxtaposition of islands hereabouts reflects the layout of the Egyptian pyramids!?

Strike inland in a couple of hundred yards, after the minor headland opposite Fidra (at the end of the plantation) on a good path, passing a signed path on your left which runs along the seaward side of another plantation, reaching a car park and turning right on the John Muir Way, inland of a narrow tree belt. Through the trees lie a series of huge new houses in this most improbable of locations. They retail for a good deal more than the proverbial King's Ransom, but I doubt they would do too well on sustainability criteria… After 300 yards the path curves around gently to the left and then leaves the tree belt to the right on a good straight track across the fields in the direction of the village which you can see ahead of you. Continue right into Dirleton passing the church (see box) and arrive at the village green of this very attractive conservation village with the castle grounds on the other side of the main road. Right on the junction with the main road is the appealing **Castle Inn** 5. Another upmarket venue catering for the well-heeled locals and visi-

Architectural confection opposite the Ship

tors alike, the place has a good reputation for its food and is frequently busy. Caledonian Deuchars IPA and a guest is the cask ale choice. Last food orders are at 9pm except for winter Sundays (6pm). Buses leave for North Berwick (and on the other side of the road, back to Gullane) nearby. Ask in the pub if you need directions.

Alternative inland route (see map)

An easier if less scenic route to the Castle Inn follows the John Muir Way. Simply walk east along the main road from Gullane, and about a kilometre (just over half a mile) beyond the end of the village a pleasant path strikes off left through the woods by Archerfield lodge as the road bends right. Follow this track for another half mile or so as it leads down and left towards the house, striking off right (sign) just before reaching the house on a track running east for another three quarters of a mile straight into Dirleton by the village green. The church is a short distance down to the left whilst the Castle Inn is a few yards along on the right.

Link route to North Berwick – west to east (see map)

The easiest and most scenic way to link the two routes is simply by following the shore at the point where the coast route above diverges inland near Fidra. You'll reach the North Berwick circuit at the wall by the West Links Golf Course described in the town circuit.

PUB INFORMATION

1 Auld Hoose
19 Forth St, North Berwick,
EH39 4HX
01620 892 692
www.caskandbarrel.co.uk
Opening Hours: 11 (12 Sun)-11
(midnight Sat)
CAMRA Regional Inventory

2 Ship Inn
7/9 Quality St, North Berwick,
EH39 4HJ
01620 890676
Opening Hours: 11-11
(midnight Thu-Sat)

3 Nether Abbey Hotel
20 Dirleton Av, North Berwick,
EH39 4BQ
01620 892802
www.netherabbey.co.uk
Opening Hours: 11-11 (midnight
Thu; 1am Fri & Sat)

4 Old Clubhouse
East Links Rd, Gullane, EH31 2AF
01620 842 008
www.oldclubhouse.com
Opening Hours: 11 (12.30 Sun)-11
(midnight Thu-Sat)

5 Castle Inn
Manse Rd, Dirleton, EH39 5EP
01620 850 221
www.castleinndirleton.com
Opening Hours: 11 (12.30 Sun)-11

A Dunbar Coastal Trail

WALK INFORMATION

Start: West Barns village

Finish: Dunbar

Access: Trains to Dunbar and bus to West Barns, or the X6 or X8 bus from St. Andrew Square (west side) alighting at West Barns

Distance: 3.5 miles (6km)

Key attractions: Ruins of Dunbar Castle, John Muir Country Park, Belhaven brewery, Birthplace of John Muir

The pubs: Mason's Arms, The Rocks, Volunteer Arms

Links: to walk 22

This is an excellent coastal walk full of interest which, if you do the full round, offers a mixture of coastal marshes, sandy bays and rocky headlands as well as impressive sandstone cliffs and panoramic sea views throughout. Out in the Firth of Forth the volcanic plug of the Bass Rock is your almost constant if rather distant companion. Save this walk for a bright and preferably warm day otherwise you'll need to wrap up well. I recommend tackling this walk by starting at West Barns rather than in Dunbar: this way it'll be easier to plan your return transport. For a shorter version of the walk simply alight from the bus in Belhaven and head straight for the Masons Arms, but check the times first – it doesn't open until midday!

West Barns is a small linear village in which you'll be hard pushed to get lost! From Edinburgh either take a train to Dunbar and then walk down to the High Street and pick up a bus alighting at the West Barns Inn in the village, a ten minute ride. Alternatively take the X6 or X8 bus from St. Andrew Square (west side) alighting at West Barns, returning by bus or by train from Dunbar at the finish of your walk. From the bus stop near the pub walk along to the river bridge at the western end of the village and crossing the river (the Biel Water) pick up a path immediately on the right which follows the stream for about 200 yards before bearing off left and heading out over a flat landscape of freshwater marsh towards the sea. Very soon you'll reach a path junction with a car park fields and just over on your left – there are public toilets in another 75 yards or so and opposite these a very good interpretation board with a detailed map.

Dunbar Castle ruins

left: **John Muir museum** right: **Masons Arms**

If you're here in good time and feeling energetic it's possible to continue straight ahead and complete a circuit around the wooded plantation and out to the estuary of the River Tyne, part of the John Muir Country Park, which will eventually bring you in a loop back to your starting point. Otherwise at this junction take the track on your right signposted John Muir Way, which follows the shore back towards Dunbar. Spring tides come very close to the path in places, but if the tide is out it will hardly feel as if you are on the coast for there are wide marshes here and beyond them the broad sands of Belhaven Bay. Bear a little way inland after a few minutes to re-cross the Biel Water on a metal footbridge and turn left, continuing on the good path past a small caravan park by a lagoon on your right before

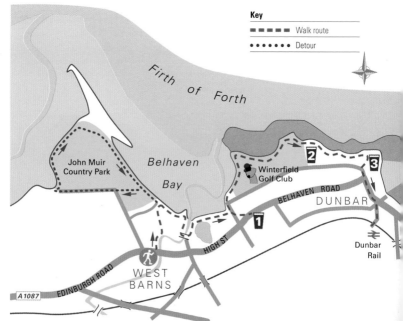

Key

━ ━ ━ ━ Walk route

•••••• Detour

Firth of Forth

John Muir Country Park

Belhaven Bay

Winterfield Golf Club

BELHAVEN ROAD

DUNBAR

Dunbar Rail

HIGH ST

WEST BARNS

EDINBURGH ROAD

A1087

reaching Belhaven where the John Muir Way joins a quiet lane. Now turn right onto this lane then take the first left – before you reach the main road – and walk down past some attractive houses to join the main road just 50 yards short of our first pub, the **Masons Arms** .

Inside the Rocks

It's a traditional village local with a plain but comfortable public bar featuring a roaring fire in winter. To the left is a formal dining room with an open kitchen adjacent. Not surprisingly for what is, in all but name, the tap for the well known brewery nearby (see below) the Masons always offers a beer from Belhaven, alongside one or two guests, frequently from smaller Scottish breweries. There's a good food menu served from 12-2 and evenings from 6-9. As to Belhaven's most celebrated attraction, you can see it by looking out the windows at the rear of the pub! It's been established here since at least 1719. Brewery tours are possible and more information is available at www.belhaven.co.uk/tours, or by phoning 01368 869200. Plan in advance though, don't expect to just turn up on spec!

The lane down to the brewery is just to your left when you leave the Masons Arms; otherwise

retrace your steps to rejoin the John Muir Way, this time continuing in the other direction down the lane which soon reverts to a path. A curious (*very* curious, depending upon the state of the tide) footbridge on the shore offers access at low tide to the sand bars across the river mouth, while our path skirts around the golf course with its prominent red sandstone clubhouse on the headland. The path hugs the coast, climbing the red sandstone cliffs that show evidence of the impact of years of weathering. It's worth pausing to admire the panoramic views, including the Bass Rock out in the Firth of Forth. Famous for its enormous colonies of gannets, this extinct volcanic plug is 350' (107m) high and for over a century has had a lighthouse which you will be able to make out on a clear day. A little further along the coast your next port of call comes into view and it's very difficult to miss. **The Rocks** **2** is a prominent sandstone hotel set about 100 yards inland from the coast path among the greens and gardens on the outskirts of Dunbar itself. Primarily a hotel it has a comfortable and well-appointed bar with classy wooden floor and a real fire. Most importantly, The Rocks offers two well-kept

The Bass Rock broods over Belhaven Bay

Shore platform near Dunbar

real ales, usually Caledonian Deuchars IPA and a rotating guest. Service is friendly and efficient and, as you would expect, good quality food is available.

Rejoin the coast path which rises, falls, twists and turns across Dunbar's complex coastal geology for the short walk into town. The remains of Dunbar Castle quickly come into view: this was once one of Scotland's most impregnable fortresses, with a history going back to Roman times. Formerly a Northumbrian stronghold although later captured by the Scots, it was then repeatedly attacked by the English. Today it is a fragile and dangerous ruin providing a picturesque backdrop to Dunbar Harbour, which in good weather is well worth the very short detour (see below).

The big glass building on the cliff top is the swimming pool. Head just inland beyond this and slightly to your left (or cut through the car park) to join Victoria Street which runs down towards the harbour, and it's almost impossible to miss the **Volunteer Arms** 3, a tall red building with a sturdy freestanding pub sign in front. A very traditional cosy bar awaits you inside with a small snug on the left as you enter. The walls are decorated with fishing and

lifeboat memorabilia, whilst the ceiling above the bar is decked out in pump clips of beers which have appeared at the Volunteer – this is a pub that takes its ales seriously and offers a choice of two constantly changing beers. Upstairs there's a dining area offering a good menu with an emphasis on seafood. From here it's just a couple of minutes walk down to the harbour. In fact there are two harbours – the main one is called the Victoria, whilst to the right is the older and original Cromwell Harbour.

If you've done your homework you'll know your bus/train times before you arrived here: it's less than a five minute walk back up Victoria Street to the High Street, where you bear left into a wide and attractive thoroughfare lined with handsome buildings. Here is John Muir's birthplace, a short distance up on the right (free admission). The bus stop is another hundred yards, beyond the road junction, and the station up beyond the church at the top of the hill. ▶▶ LINK ◀◀

> **PUB INFORMATION**

1 Masons Arms
8 High St, Belhaven, Dunbar,
EH42 1NP
01368 863700
Opening Hours: 12-3, 5-11;
12-midnight Fri & Sat; 12.30-11
Sun

2 The Rocks
Marine Rd, Dunbar, EH42 1AR
01368 862287
www.experiencetherocks.co.uk
Opening Hours: 11 (12.30
Sun)-11

3 Volunteer Arms
17 Victoria St, Dunbar, EH42 1HP
01368 862278
Opening Hours: 12-11 (midnight
Thu; 1am Fri & Sat); 12.30-mid-
night Sun

▶▶ LINK ◀◀ Walk 22 **Georgian Haddington** (page 119) the bus back to Edinburgh goes via Haddington; but both routes together would make a long day, so best tackled in summer by energetic walkers/drinkers!

Heritage Pubs

route 25 – The Best of Edinburgh's Pub Architecture

top: **Sportsman window from the Café Royal** bottom: **Tiles interior**

The Best of Edinburgh's Pub Architecture

ROUTE INFORMATION

Start/Finish: Waverley Steps or St. Andrew Square

Access: Trains to Waverley, buses to Waverley Bridge and Princes Street

The pubs: Athletic Arms, Bennet's Bar, Station Bar, Barony Bar, Leslie's Bar, Café Royal, Abbotsford Bar, Dome Bar, Kenilworth, Oxford Bar

In a city of superlatives, the pubs also play their part, with some of the finest pub architecture in Britain found here. This is a subjective selection of some of the best, which will delight lovers of classic pub interiors. Most but not all of the pubs in this tour, which will require bus journeys in places, appear elsewhere in this book; and although you'll be able to get a glass of real ale in the majority of them, the main criteria here is the fittings, and/or the antiquity, so the pub descriptions have more architectural detail. There are more pubs on this route than any other, so in the spirit of encouraging responsible drinking, either take the route in sections, or at least spread it over a long day and ration yourself!

Café Royal interior

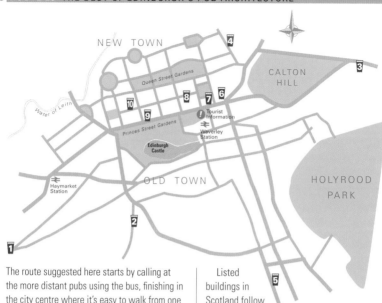

The route suggested here starts by calling at the more distant pubs using the bus, finishing in the city centre where it's easy to walk from one to the next. Needless to say you can take them in any order you like! It's a good idea to equip yourself with a map of the city if you're traveling to the pubs on the bus for the first time; and/or to ask for help from the driver. You may find a visit to the Historic Scotland online booklet on pub architecture useful before undertaking this tour: see www.historic-scotland.gov.uk/raising-the-bar-pubs-booklet.pdf

Listed buildings in Scotland follow a similar concept to those south of the border. Here the categories are as follows:

Category A – buildings of national importance
Category B – buildings of regional importance
Category C(s) – buildings of local importance

Start by taking a No. 1 or 34 bus to the **Athletic Arms** 1 in Dalry (walk 11). You'll pass the modern boxy retail development

left: **Athletic Arms oak bar**   right: **Bennet's Bar mirrors**

on Fountainbridge of the old brewery site on the right and then the road merges into the Western Approach Road. The pub is prominently on the apex across the street here. Ask for the 'Diggers' as the Athletic is known locally in view of its location between two cemeteries. The bar is at the foot of a bold 5-storey Victorian tenement block dating to about 1889, and is listed Category C(s). The interior is exceptional and relatively little altered from a scheme of about 1900, except for the removal of screens and partitions more recently by new owners Scottish & Newcastle. Red leather benches line the outer walls, and the slim, free-standing central oak bar unit is a real star here. A pub where for years the McEwan's 80/- was lined up on the bar by the gallon, the place still gets busy on match days even though like a lot of classic pubs it is quieter than it was. Real ales: Caledonian Deuchars IPA, Stewart 80/- and two guests. Don't miss the classic Aitken founts on the bar counter.

Moving on, we need bus 35 heading back into town along the southern (Angle Park Terrace) side of the pub, aiming for Tollcross, the big five-

The serving hatch at the tiny jug bar at Bennet's

ways junction at the southern end of Lothian Road. The bus follows the one way system from Fountainbridge and turns right into Lothian Road from Morrison Street, continuing up to Tollcross. Alight here and either walk the 300 yards up Home Street to the King's Theatre, or wait at the stop and take bus 10, 11, 15, or 16 for one more stop which brings you out on Home Street just beyond the Tollcross junction.

Almost adjacent the stop, on the left by the King's Theatre is **Bennet's Bar 2** (see walk 8). Listed at Grade B, many would say that after the Café Royal this is Edinburgh's second finest interior. Certainly it has changed little in over a century, apart from the regrettable removal of a couple of small snugs, once again by Scottish & Newcastle. The star turns here are many: even before you get inside you should admire the top-notch leaded, stained glass window and door panels advertising 'Jeffrey's Lager & W & J Jenkinson's Bottled Beers & Aerated Waters'. The interior features some wonderful tile work (with paintings by the famous London firm of Simpson & Sons on tiles from the famous

Barony Bar

old Severnside works of Maw & Co). The mirrors are of matching quality, including a venerable selection of old brewery mirrors as well as the inlaid ones. Behind the servery the original gantry survives, with four large spirit casks. The tiny jug bar is quite superb, and

Unique wooden screen, Leslie's Bar

another remarkable survival; it's a pity that the licensees don't find a better way to make use of it other than as a store for boxes and such like. The sturdy bar counter retains two working brass water taps whilst down below the old marble spittoon is still there. In contrast to all this splendour the cask ale selection is limited: Caledonian Deuchars and 80. There is a fabulous selection of over 100 malt whiskies though!

Return to the bus stop at Tollcross and take the 35 bus once again, down the Royal Mile and alighting in about 25 minutes at the first stop on Easter Road just beyond the *Regent* at the top of Abbey Mount, two stops beyond Holyrood Palace. The *Regent* is not on our itinerary, but walk back to it and turn left to join London Road in two or three minutes. Just beyond, on the right, just before the rail bridge, is the **Station Bar 3** on Cadzow Place. This classic, unspoiled working man's bar stands at the foot of a plain but dignified four-storey tenement building. It has no real ale but is well worth a visit for its unaltered interior scheme from what feels like another era. Although unlisted, this is exactly the sort of pub which is now increasingly rare, yet overlooked by the listing system with its focus upon classy and 'top end' architecture rather than plain but unadulterated schemes, which are ironically all the rarer. Pride of place goes to the tiny jug and bottle (off sales) compartment on the right; but the public bar has its original counter with a four bay gantry behind. Don't miss (as if you could) the absolutely massive 'Dryborough's Pale & Mild Ales' mirror.

Drinks? You're on your own...

Now take a bus back towards the city centre from the nearby stop on this side of the street. Nos 4, 15/15A, 26 and 44 will drop you at York Place. This is the first stop beyond the big roundabout at the top of Leith Walk where the bus takes the second exit. Map in hand, cross the street and walk back a few yards to the junction, and look for Broughton Street running away downhill on the left. The Category B listed **Barony Bar 4** is at No. 85 on the right down here (see walk 3). The whole block is a fine 'B' listed tenement from the early 19th century although the Barony frontage and interior is late Victorian, by John M Forrester who designed five pubs in this part of the city. The classy interior is dominated by some fine tiled panels and good timber work on the chimneypieces, bar and gantry. Real ales are Caledonian Deuchars IPA, Black Sheep Bitter and guest beers.

Coming out of the Barony pick up a No. 8 bus from one of the stops on the same side of the street. This will take you up via St. Andrew Square and across the city centre into the Southside. Consult your street map: you want to alight at the stop by the junction of Minto Street and Middleby Street. Cross the road and walk down Middleby Street, turning left at the end, then right into West Mayfield, which quickly brings you out to another main road, Ratcliffe Terrace. Turn right here and a little way up on the right is **Leslie's Bar 5**.

Another great late Victorian Edinburgh bar, in a kind of classical revival style, and listed at Grade B, again like so many of the city's best pubs it occupies the bottom of a handsome tenement (see walk 13). It's the work of P. L. Henderson, probably the most prolific, and arguably one of the best pub architects Scotland has seen. Named after an early licensee, the place has a very large island bar, but what makes it unique is the wooden screen on one side, punctuated by a series of low windows, very much like old fashioned ticket booths. There is nothing quite like this anywhere else although its function was similar to the snob screens in some English pubs, to afford some privacy to the richer customers who didn't want to be looked up and down by the hoi-polloi. At the front of the pub on the same (left) side is a small snug. On the far end of the bar counter is another wooden gantry with glazed panels and decorative carving. There are panelled dados throughout, dating back to the 1950s, including two small open sided rooms: that at front leading off bar was formerly a neighbouring shop, and at the rear, another snug. Finally, don't forget to look upwards, to the wonderful ceiling set off by an ornate plaster cornice above an original lincrusta frieze. All pretty breathtaking. Beers are Caledonian Deu-

Tile detail from Café Royal

chars IPA, Stewart 80/-, Timothy Taylor Landlord, plus two changing guests.

To head back into the city centre, either wait opposite for a 42 or 67 which drop you back in the centre of town, or retrace your steps to Minto Street which has far more buses; services 3, 8, 29, 31, 37 and 47 will ferry you back to Princes Street, where you should alight at the stop by Waverley Steps, the first one after turning left off North Bridge. Use the map on walk 1 to make your way to the **Café Royal** 6, in West Register Street. Listed at Grade A, this mid Victorian pub is surely in terms of the richness of the fittings top of the league of Edinburgh pub interiors. This is one of Edinburgh's most famous pubs. Whether it's the marble floor, the enchanting Doulton tiled murals depicting famous inventors, the original fireplace, or the ornate and compartmented ceiling above a rich frieze, you cannot help but be impressed with the richness

Café Royal interior

of the decor. Even the newer work like the island serving counter and the gantry is good quality. The Oyster Bar, at the west end of the ground floor, lies behind a superb walnut screen with inset mirror panels. You ought to look in here just to admire the lovely marble bar counter and the stained glass windows, second to none in an Edinburgh pub. The room upstairs (see walk 1) is no longer part of the pub but also has some very good quality work. Cask ales on offer are Caledonian Deuchars IPA and guest beers.

Now walk back out to St. Andrew Square, crossing and passing *Tiles*, no mean interior itself, and across South St. David Street to enter Rose Street almost opposite Sainsbury's. The next building beyond is the **Abbotsford Bar** 7 (walk 6). It's a handsome red sandstone corner pub with a 'witch's hat' turret not dissimilar to the trademark design of the old Brickwood's brewery in Portsmouth. It is another work of P. L. Henderson (see Leslie's Bar, above). Inside, it's in many ways perhaps the classic island bar pub, with the 'island' itself of considerable substance. There's a lavishly carved mahogany superstructure on the counter, supported on paired columns and with a pot shelf running along the top. The dado around the walls has inset mirrors and larger brewery mirrors above,

all under a superb compartmented ceiling. In the far left corner is the original snack counter, an unusual survivor still in use at lunchtimes, and itself sporting an impressive back gantry and mirrored panels. Originally there was a smoke room and lounge at the rear of the main ground floor room but when the first floor was acquired by the pub in the 1970s for a restaurant, these rooms were converted to accommodate the staircase. Nonetheless as an unspoiled example of the late nineteenth century pub at its best this is hard to beat, although only listed at Category B. Cask beer range is excellent too with five changing ales dispensed from one of the city's finest surviving array of Aitken founts.

Return to St. Andrew Square, but this time keep left and take the next turning left into George Street. Here, a couple of minutes down on the left, is the **Dome** 8. This massive building, one of the very few freestanding buildings in the first New Town, was a former bank, built in 1844 in the form of a Graeco-Roman temple, and the work of David Rhind (1808-1883) who was employed as the architect by the Commercial Bank of Scotland. The impressive frontage is based on an earlier scheme by William Playfair for the Surgeons Hall, (the old Physicians' Hall was demolished to make way for this building),

left: **The bar gantry at the Abbotsford**   centre: **The Dome's magnificent ceiling**

Kenilworth bar

but inside you'll be blown away by the magnificent Telling Hall, a Greek cross with arched ceilings and coffered central dome. The columns were originally made of wood, but in 1885 they were refaced in grey and red veined marble, with black granite bases and bronze capitals. The amalgamation of the bank with the Royal Bank of Scotland meant that the building eventually became redundant and was converted to the pub it is to-day in the early 1990s. Not surprisingly the place is listed Category A; the only pity in this building of superlatives is that they haven't cottoned on to real ale: if you're very lucky the Caledonian Deuchars IPA may be on, otherwise…

Continue along George Street and take the first left, Hanover Street, at the next junction, then first right back into the pedestrianised Rose Street. Walk down until you reach the **Kenilworth 9** on your left at No. 152 (see walk 6). Another impressive island-bar pub, it

has recently been deservedly upgraded to a Category A listing. The detailed late Victorian timber front is probably down to Thomas Purves Marwick, who drew inspiration for the neo-Jacobean interior styling from prolific pub architect P. L. Henderson, who himself may have had a large hand in the design of the interior. The island bar layout was Marwick's work from a remodelling around the turn of the twentieth century, and it was at this time that the flat above the pub was also acquired creating the unusual double height interior. The walls are covered in blue and white Minton tiles, some restored and/or replaced in a good quality refurbishment in the 1960s. Don't overlook too the splendid mahogany island bar with some quality carving. Note the huge Drybrough's mirror, not the first we've seen on this tour. Cask ales are Caledonian Deuchars IPA and 80 and three guest beers.

The final stop of this marathon is close by: exit

bottom right: **Minton tiles in the Kenilworth** top right: **Mirror in the Kenilworth**

The unchanged Oxford bar

the Kenilworth and walk the few yards west to join Castle Street, where you turn left and cross George Street before taking the first left beyond which is Young Street. The **Oxford Bar** 10 is a few yards ahead. After the stunning architecture you've seen on this circuit, the 'Ox' is something different – here is a plain, basic and wonderfully intact old drinking shop from the early nineteenth century with few embellishments; but for all that one of the city's great pubs. Setting the scene, the opaque windows with some Bernard's brewery lettering; inside, a tiny stand-up bar to

the left, with no room for tables or seats save a couple of tiny window benches; up some steps to a larger sitting room, a no-frills place for conversation, with no distractions save the interesting old pictures on the walls (see walk 6). The 1950s brick fireplace looks a little incongruous. Cask beers are Caledonian Deuchars IPA and two guests. The 'Ox' is listed Category B.

Princes Street with its connections to almost anywhere is very close: retrace your steps to Castle Street and turning right follow your eyes towards the castle itself.

PUB INFORMATION

1 Athletic Arms (Diggers)
1-3 Angle Park Ter, Edinburgh,
EH11 2JX
0131 337 3822
Opening Hours: 11 (12.30 Sun)-1am
CAMRA Regional Inventory

2 Bennet's Bar
8 Leven St, Edinburgh, EH3 9LG
0131 229 5143
Opening Hours: 11-12.30am (1am Thu-Sat); 12.30-11.30 Sun
CAMRA National Inventory (Part 1)

3 Station Bar
21 Cadzow Pl, Edinburgh, EH7 5SN
0131 661 2855
Opening Hours: 11-12.30am (1am Thu-Sat); 12.30-11.30 Sun
CAMRA Regional Inventory (Part 1)

4 Barony Bar
81/85 Broughton St, Edinburgh,
EH1 3RJ
0131 558 2874
Opening Hours: 11 (12.30 Sun)-midnight (1am Fri & Sat)
CAMRA Regional Inventory (Part 2)

5 Leslie's Bar
45/47 Ratcliffe Ter, Edinburgh,
EH9 1SU
0131 667 7205
www.lesliesbar.com
Opening Hours: 11-11 (11.30 Thu; 12.30am Fri & Sat); 12.30-11.30 Sun
CAMRA National Inventory (Part 1)

6 Café Royal
19 West Register St, Edinburgh,
EH2 2AA
0131 556 1884
www.caferoyal.org.uk
Opening Hours: 11 (12.30 Sun)-11 (midnight Thu; 1am Fri & Sat)
CAMRA National Inventory (Part 2)

7 Abbotsford Bar
3-5 Rose St, Edinburgh, EH2 2PR
0131 225 5276
www.theabbotsford.com
Opening Hours:
11(12.30 Sun)-11(midnight Fri & Sat)
CAMRA National Inventory (Part 1)

8 Dome Bar
14 George St, Edinburgh, EH2 2PF
0131 624 8624
www.thedomeedinburgh.com
Opening Hours: 12-late

9 Kenilworth Arms
152/154 Rose St, Edinburgh,
EH2 3JD
0131 226 1773
Opening Hours: 10-1am
CAMRA National Inventory (Part 2)

10 Oxford Bar
8 Young St, Edinburgh, EH2 4JB
0131 539 7119
www.oxfordbar.com
Opening Hours: 11-midnight (1am Thu-Sat); 12.30-11 Sun
CAMRA National Inventory (Part 1)

Barony Bar tiles

Accommodation

Edinburgh is fortunate to have a number of accommodation options for all budgets – from five star hotels and luxury apartments to student halls of residence, and a few campsites and caravan parks. Visit Scotland has a star rating scheme for accommodation which ranges from ★ for acceptable to ★ ★ ★ ★ ★ for exceptional, and many hotels and b&bs around Edinburgh will display a blue plaque with their star rating. The Scottish Tourist Board's website www.visitscotland.com has a useful accommodation search feature.

Beer, Bed and Breakfast:

In addition to this, a number of real ale pubs and bars, some of which are featured on the routes, also offer accommodation. Below is a selection of accommodation options where you can find a beer to go with your bed and breakfast.

Bank Hotel

1 South Bridge, Edinburgh, EH1 1LL
0131 622 6800
www.festival-inns.co.uk
Double/twin from £94/night

Hampton Hotel

14 Corstorphine Road, Edinburgh, EH12 6HN
0131 337 1130
www.hamptonhotel.co.uk
Double from £80/night

Best Western Braid Hills Hotel

(Buckstone Bistro)
134 Braid Rd, Edinburgh, EH10 6JD
0131 447 8888
www.braidhillshotel.co.uk
Double from £100/night b&b

Self-catering apartment in Morningside

c/o Cumberland Bar 1-3 Cumberland St, Edinburgh, EH3 6RT
0131 558 3134
www.cumberlandbar.co.uk
2-person s/c apartment from £60/night (min 2 nights)

Riccarton Arms

198 Lanark Rd West, Currie, EH14 5NX
0131 449 2230
www.thericcartonarms.co.uk

Hawes Inn

7 Newhalls Road, South Queensferry, EH30 9TA
0131 331 1990
www.vintageinn.co.uk/thehawesinnsouthqueensferry
Double from £67/night

Castle Inn

Manse Rd, Dirleton, EH39 5EP
01620 850 221
www.castleinndirleton.com
Double/twin from £80/night b&b

Nether Abbey Hotel

20 Dirleton Av, North Berwick, EH39 4BQ
01620 892802
www.netherabbey.co.uk
Double/twin from £95/night b&b

The Rocks

Marine Rd, Dunbar, EH42 1AR
01368 862287
experiencetherocks.co.uk
Double/twin from £70/night b&b

Camping:

Mortonhall Caravan & Camping Park

(Stable Bar)
38 Mortonhall Gate, Frogston Road, Edinburgh, EH16 6TJ
0131 664 1533
http://www.meadowhead.co.uk/MortonhallHome.aspx
From £10.50 pppn

Stable Bar, Mortonhall

Transport

Edinburgh is a compact city with a wealth of public transport options, both for arriving in the city and getting around – so you can leave your car at home. All the routes in this book are accessible by public transport from the city centre, and transport options are detailed at the beginning of each walk.

Getting there:

Scotland's capital city is well connected to the rest of the UK, with direct train services from London, Birmingham, Glasgow and Aberdeen all terminating at Edinburgh Waverley. Journey time from London can be under 4½ hours and many rail operators offer significant discounts for advance bookings.

Edinburgh airport is five miles west of the city centre and is served by budget airlines from many UK and European hubs. Lothian Buses number 100 airport express bus provides a regular shuttle service between the airport and Haymarket and Waverley stations, and a link from the airport to the new tram network is expected to become operational in 2012. Glasgow airport is also well served by budget operators and flights to Glasgow are often cheaper than those to Edinburgh. Glasgow city centre is under an hour's train journey from Edinburgh, as well as offering a wide variety of visitor attractions in its own right.

Getting around:

Bus

Lothian Buses provide the best way of getting around Edinburgh, with a comprehensive network of routes within the city, and a night bus service that ensures 24-hour transport options. Relevant bus routes are given at the start of each walk, and route maps are available from the Tourist Information centre at Waverley Steps as well as the Lothian Buses Travelshops on Waverley Bridge and Shandwick Place. A Lothian Bus map is printed on page 146-7.

Fares are a flat rate of £1.20 (or £1.10 from an on-street ticket machine) to anywhere in the city, whilst a £3 day ticket gives you unlimited bus travel for a day. Be warned though that you'll need the correct money for your ticket if you buy on the bus as Lothian bus drivers don't give change. More information can be found at www.lothianbuses.com.

For destinations slightly further afield, services operated by First Group serve Gullane, North Berwick, Haddington and Dunbar, as well as numerous routes within and around Edinburgh. Route and timetable information can be found at www.firstgroup.com.

Train:

Edinburgh is served by Waverley and Haymarket stations. First ScotRail operates local train services to both

Lothian buses are a quick and easy way of getting around the city

Cyclists at Cramond

Kirkcaldy and Linlithgow out of both Edinburgh stations, as well as to numerous other destinations in Scotland.

Tram:

Edinburgh's new tram system is expected to start operating in 2012 with one line running east/west across the city and connecting Leith's Ocean Terminal to the airport.

Bike:

Despite appearances, Edinburgh is a very cycle-friendly city, with numerous cycle routes and cycle-friendly modifications to road layouts. A useful map is available from Edinburgh cycling organisation Spokes www.spokes.org.uk which has details of all Edinburgh cycle routes and traffic-calmed roads, as well as details of other cycle routes in the Lothians and Borders. Edinburgh has numerous cycle shops and bikes can be rented from Cycle Scotland www.cyclescotland.co.uk and Biketrax www.biketrax.co.uk. Many of the routes in this book can be adapted or extended for cyclists – for example the towpath along the Union Canal connects Edinburgh's West End pubs (walks 11 and 12) to those along the Water of Leith (walk 16), whilst a Sunday blast through the Innocent Railway Tunnel and around Queen's Drive to Duddingston (walk 14) won't be forgotten in a hurry.

For a laid-back (purely in the physical sense of the word) view of Edinburgh, David Gardiner,

Edinburgh's recumbent bike and trike expert runs tours around the city, taking in real ale pubs including the Sheep Heid Inn in Duddingston and the Old Chain Pier in Leith. See www.laid-back-bikes.co.uk for more details.

Car:

With a wealth of public transport options and a fleet of black cabs operating, there isn't much call to use a car in Edinburgh. Parking, in particular, can be difficult and a network of one-way roads can confuse the unwary. Information on parking can be found on Edinburgh city council's website www.edinburgh.gov.uk.

GLOSSARY	
Geography:	
Brae	slope
Brig	bridge
Burn	slow-moving stream
Court	courtyard surrounded on all sides by buildings
Dooocot	dovecot
Firth	estuary
Howff	haunt or meeting-place
Kirk	church
Lade	leat or mill race (channel of water leading to mill wheel)
Land	tenement block of flats
Law	rounded hill
Loan	common ground
Pend	archway
(Bus) stance	Scottish alternative to bus stand
Setts	squared cobbles
Vennel	lane or passageway
Wynd	narrow thoroughfare, open from end to end

Beer styles

You can deepen your appreciation of cask ale and get to grips with the Edinburgh's traditional beers with this run-down on the main styles available.

Scottish Beers

As a result of temperament and temperature, the Scots have for centuries brewed ales that are distinctively different from those made south of the border. A cold climate requires beers that are hearty and warming; as a result Scottish ales tend to be dark, often brewed with the addition of heavily roasted malts, oats and other cereals, and rich with unfermented sugar. The traditional, classic styles are 60/- or Light, low in strength and so-called even when dark in colour; 70/- or Heavy; 80/- or Export; and the strong 90/- Wee Heavy, similar to a barley wine. The names date from the 19th-century method of stating the wholesale price for beer per barrel in shillings. Scottish ales are brewed in a different way from English ones as the Scottish climate was not conducive to the development of a hop industry and brewers used them sparingly or not at all. Because of this the copper boil lasts for a shorter time – as fewer hops are used, it is important not to boil away the delicate aromas and fla-

Shepherd Neame's Early Bird, a golden ale

vours of the plant. Scottish brewers still produce the traditional Heavies and Exports, but many of the new craft breweries produce beers lighter in colour and with generous hop rates – with Caledonian Deuchars IPA and Harviestoun Bitter & Twisted at the forefront of the style.

Golden Ales

This new style of pale, well-hopped and quenching beer developed in the 1980s as independent brewers attempted to win younger drinkers from heavily-promoted lager brands. The first in the field were Exmoor Gold and Hop Back Summer Lightning, though many micros and regionals now make their versions of the style. Strengths will range from 3.5% to 5%. The hallmark will be the biscuity and juicy malt character derived from pale malts, underscored by tart citrus fruit and peppery hops, often with the addition of hints of vanilla and sweetcorn. Above all, such beers are quenching and served cool.

IPA and Pale Ale

India Pale Ale changed the face of brewing early in the 19th century. The new technologies of the Industrial Revolution enabled brewers to use pale malts to fashion beers that were genuinely golden or pale bronze in colour. First brewed in London and Burton-on-Trent for the colonial market, IPAs were strong in alcohol and high in hops: the

Caledonian 80

Harviestoun Bitter & Twisted

preservative character of the hops helped keep the beers in good condition during long sea journeys. Beers with less alcohol and hops were developed for the domestic market and were known as Pale Ale. Today Pale Ale is usually a bottled version of Bitter, though historically the styles are different. Marston's Pedigree is an example of Burton Pale Ale, not Bitter, while the same brewery's Old Empire is a fascinating interpretation of a Victorian IPA. So-called IPAs with strengths of around 3.5% are not true to style. Look for juicy malt, citrus fruit and a big spicy, peppery, bitter hop character, with strengths of 4% upwards.

Bitter   IPA

Bitter

Towards the end of the 19th century, brewers built large estates of tied pubs. They moved away from vatted beers stored for many months and developed 'running beers' that could be served after a few days' storage in pub cellars. Draught Mild was a 'running beer' along with a new type that was dubbed Bitter by drinkers. Bitter grew out of Pale Ale but was generally deep bronze to copper in colour due to the use of slightly darker malts such as crystal that give the beer fullness of palate. Best is a stronger version of Bitter but there is considerable crossover. Bitter falls into the 3.4% to 3.9% band, with Best Bitter 4% upwards but a number of brewers label their ordinary Bitters 'Best'. A further development of Bitter comes in the shape of Extra or Special Strong Bitters of 5% or more: familiar examples of this style include Fuller's ESB and Greene King Abbot. With ordinary Bitter, look for a spicy, peppery and grassy hop character, a powerful bitterness, tangy fruit and juicy and nutty malt. With Best and Strong Bitters, malt and fruit character will tend to dominate but hop aroma and bitterness are still crucial to the style, often achieved by 'late hopping' in the brewery or adding hops to casks as they leave for pubs.

Mild

Mild was once the most popular style of beer but was overtaken by Bitter from the 1950s. It was developed in the 18th and 19th centuries as a less aggressively bitter style of beer than porter and stout. Early Milds were much stronger that modern interpretations, which tend to fall in the 3% to 3.5% category, though there are stronger versions, such as Gale's Festival Mild and Sarah Hughes' Dark Ruby. Mild ale is usually dark brown in colour, due to the use of well-roasted malts or roasted barley, but there are paler versions, such as Banks's Original, Timothy Taylor's Golden Best and McMullen's AK. Look for rich malty aromas and flavours with hints of dark fruit, chocolate, coffee and caramel and a gentle underpinning of hop bitterness.

Old Ale

Old Ale recalls the type of beer brewed before the Industrial Revolution, stored for months or even years in unlined wooden vessels known as tuns. The beer would pick up some lactic sourness as a result of wild yeasts, lactobacilli and tannins in the wood. The result was a beer dubbed 'stale' by drinkers: it was one of the components of the early, blended Porters. The style has re-emerged in recent years, due primarily to the fame of Theakston's Old Peculier, Gale's Prize Old Ale and Thomas Hardy's Ale, the last saved from oblivion by O'Hanlon's Brewery in Devon. Old Ales, contrary to expectation, do not have to be especially strong: they can be no more than 4% alcohol, though the Gale's and O'Hanlon's versions are considerably stronger. Neither do they have to be dark: Old Ale can be pale and burst with lush sappy malt, tart fruit and spicy hop notes. Darker versions will have a more profound malt character with powerful hints of roasted grain, dark fruit, polished leather and fresh tobacco. The hallmark of the style remains a lengthy period of maturation, often in bottle rather than bulk vessels.

Porter and Stout

Fullers 1845 bottle conditioned ale

Porter was a London style that turned the brewing industry upside down early in the 18th century. It was a dark brown beer – 19th-century versions became jet black – that was originally a blend of brown ale, pale ale and 'stale' or well-matured ale. It acquired the name Porter as a result of its popularity among London's street-market workers. The strongest versions of Porter were known as Stout Porter, reduced over the years to simply Stout. Such vast quantities of Porter and Stout flooded into Ireland from London and Bristol that a Dublin brewer named Arthur Guinness decided to fashion his own interpretation of the style. Guinness in Dublin blended some unmalted roasted barley and in so doing produced a style known as Dry Irish Stout. Restrictions on making roasted malts in Britain during World War One led to the demise of Porter and Stout and left the market to the Irish. In recent years, smaller craft brewers in Britain have rekindled an interest in the style, though in keeping with modern drinking habits, strengths have been reduced. Look for profound dark and roasted malt character with raisin and sultana fruit, espresso or cappuccino coffee, liquorice and molasses.

Barley Wine

Barley Wine is a style that dates from the 18th and 19th centuries when England was often at war with France and it was the duty of patriots, usually from the upper classes, to drink ale rather than Claret. Barley Wine had to be strong – often between 10% and 12% - and was stored for prodigious periods of as long as 18 months or two years. When country houses had their own small breweries, it was often the task of the butler to brew ale that was drunk from cut-glass goblets at the dining table. The biggest-selling Barley Wine for years was Whitbread's 10.9% Gold Label, now available only in cans. Bass's No 1 Barley Wine (10.5%) is occasionally brewed in Burton-on-Trent, stored in cask for 12 months and made available to CAMRA beer festivals. Fuller's Vintage Ale (8.5%) is a bottle-conditioned version of its Golden Pride and is brewed with different varieties of malts and hops every year. Expect massive sweet malt and ripe fruit of the pear drop, orange and lemon type, with darker fruits, chocolate and coffee if darker malts are used. Hop rates are generous and produce bitterness and peppery, grassy and floral notes.

Mild   **Stout**   **Barley wine**

Home of Deuchars IPA &
Caledonian 80/-

CALEDONIAN
BREWERY

Edinburgh's Last Remaining Brewery

Pubs index

Beer index

GLOSSARY

Beers:
Light or 60/-
low strength, similar to a mild in England
and Wales

Heavy or 70/-
session beer, similar to a bitter or
best bitter

Export or 80/-
stronger beer

Wee Heavy or 90/-
strong beer, similar to a barley wine

The Aitken founts at the Abbotsford

Books for beer lovers

CAMRA Books, the publishing arm of the Campaign for Real Ale, is the leading publisher of books on beer and pubs. Key titles include:

Good Beer Guide 2011

Editor: Roger Protz

The *Good Beer Guide* is the only guide you will ever need to find the right pint, in the right place, every time. It's the original and best-selling guide to around 4,500 pubs throughout the UK. Now in its 38th year, this annual publication is a comprehensive and informative guide to the best real ale pubs in the UK, researched and written exclusively by CAMRA members and fully updated every year.

£15.99   **ISBN 978-1-85249-272-5**

London Pub Walks

Bob Steel

A practical, pocket-sized guide enabling you to explore the English capital while never being far away from a decent pint. The book includes 30 walks around more than 180 pubs serving fine real ale, from the heart of the City and bustling West End to majestic riverside routes and the leafy Wimbledon Common. Each pub is selected for its high-quality real ale, its location and its superb architectural heritage. The walks feature more pubs than any other London pub-walk guide

£8.99   **ISBN 978-1-85249-216-8**

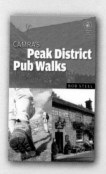

Peak District Pub Walks

Bob Steel

A practical, pocket-sized traveller's guide to some of the best pubs and best walking in the Peak District. This book features 25 walks, as well as cycle routes and local attractions, helping you see the best of Britain's oldest national park while never straying too far from a decent pint. Each route has been selected for its inspiring landscape, historical interest and welcoming pubs.

£9.99   **ISBN 978-1-85249-246-5**

BOOKS

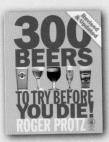

300 Beers to Try Before You Die!

Roger Protz

300 beers from around the world, handpicked by award-winning journalist, author and broadcaster Roger Protz to try before you die! A comprehensive portfolio of top beers from the smallest microbreweries in the United States to family-run British breweries and the world's largest brands. This book is indispensible for both beer novices and aficionados.

£12.99   ISBN 978-1-85249-273-1

Good Bottled Beer Guide

Jeff Evans

A pocket-sized guide for discerning drinkers looking to buy bottled real ales and enjoy a fresh glass of their favourite beers at home. The 7th edition of the *Good Bottled Beer Guide* is completely revised, updated and redesigned to showcase the very best bottled British real ales now being produced, and detail where they can be bought. Everything you need to know about bottled beers; tasting notes, ingredients, brewery details, and a glossary to help the reader understand more about them.

£12.99   ISBN 978-1-85249-262-5

Good Beer Guide Belgium

Tim Webb

The completely revised and updated 6th edition of the guide so impressive that it is acknowledged as the standard work for Belgian beer lovers, even in Belgium itself. The *Good Beer Guide Belguim* includes comprehensive advice on getting there, being there, what to eat, where to stay and how to bring beers back home. Its outline of breweries, beers and bars makes this book indispensible for both leisure and business travellers a well as for armchair drinkers looking to enjoy a selection of Belgian brews from their local beer store.

£14.99   ISBN 978-1-85249-261-8

London Heritage Pubs — An inside story

Geoff Brandwood & Jane Jephcote

The definitive guidebook to London's most unspoilt pubs. Raging from gloriously rich Victorian extravaganzas to unspoilt community street-corner locals, the pubs not only have interiors of genuine heritage value, they also have fascinating stories to tell. London Heritage pubs – An inside story is a must for anyone interested in visiting and learning about London's magnificent pubs.

£14.99   ISBN 978-1-85249-247-2

SCOTLAND'S TRUE HERITAGE PUBS

Editor: Mick Slaughter

This unique guide will lead you to 115 Scottish pubs which have historic fittings of real national significance, many of which have altered little in the past 40 years or so. Some of the featured pubs are tiny old-fashioned time-warp inns, others are magnificent Victorian drinking palaces and Art Deco masterpieces.

£6.99   ISBN 978-1-85249-242-7

Brew Your Own British Real Ale

Graham Wheeler

The perennial favourite of home-brewers, *Brew Your Own British Real Ale* is a CAMRA classic. This new edition is re-written, enhanced and updated with new recipes for contemporary and award-winning beers, as well as recipes for old favourites no longer brewed commercially. Written by home-brewing authority Graham Wheeler, *Brew Your Own British Real Ale* includes detailed brewing instructions for both novice and more advanced home-brewers, as well as comprehensive recipes for recreating some of Britain's best-loved beers at home.

£14.99   ISBN 978-1-85249-258-8

BOOKS

Order these and other CAMRA books online at
www.camra.org.uk/books,
ask at your local bookstore, or contact:
CAMRA, 230 Hatfield Road,
St Albans, AL1 4LW. Telephone 01727 867201

Find Good Beer Guide pubs on the move – anytime, anywhere!

CAMRA's two hi-tech services for beer lovers – the *Good Beer Guide Mobile Edition* and *Good Beer Guide POI* sat-nav file – offer the perfect solution to pub finding on the move.

Good Beer Guide goes mobile!

The *Good Beer Guide Mobile Edition* makes the ideal companion to the printed *Good Beer Guide*. Wherever you are, or wherever you are going, get information on local *Good Beer Guide* pubs and beers sent direct to your mobile phone.

Compatible with most mobile phones with Internet access, including the iPhone/iPod Touch, this unique service allows you to search by postcode, place name or London tube station – or it can locate your current location using GPS. Search results contain full information and descriptions for local pubs and include tasting notes for their regular beers. Interactive maps help you navigate to your destination.

To use the service, simply text **'camra'** to **07766 40 41 42**. You will then receive a text message with a web link to download the application (or, if you are an iPhone user, download the application from the App Store).

This indispensible service is **free to trial for 7 days** (excluding the iPhone/iPod Touch version) and **costs just £5** for each annual edition.

(Please note that your standard network charges apply when using this service. For more information on makes and models of phones supported, please visit: **http//m.camra.org.uk**)

Find *Good Beer Guide* pubs using satellite navigation!

The *Good Beer Guide POI* (Points of Interest) file allows users of TomTom, Garmin and Navman sat-nav systems to see the locations of all the 4,500-plus current *Good Beer Guide* pubs and plan routes to them. So, now, wherever you are, there is no excuse for not finding your nearest *Good Beer Guide* pub!

The file is simple to install and use and full instructions are provided. **Priced at just £5.00**, it is the perfect tool for any serious pub explorer. No more wasting time thumbing through road atlases or getting lost down country lanes. Navigate your way easily, every time, and make the most of Britain's best pubs.

To download the file visit: **www.camra.org.uk/gbgpoi**

It takes all sorts to Campaign for Real Ale

CAMRA, the Campaign for Real Ale, is an independent not-for-profit, volunteer-led consumer group. We promote good-quality real ale and pubs as well as lobbyin government to champion drinkers' rights and protect local pubs as centres of community life.

CAMRA has 110,000 members from all ages and backgrounds, brought together by a common belief in the issues that CAMRA deals with and their love of good quality British beer and cider. For just £20 a year — that's less than a pint a month — you can join CAMRA and enjoy the following benefits:

A monthly colour newspaper informing you about beer and pub news and detailing events and beer festivals around the country.

Free or reduced entry to over 140 national, regional and local beer festivals.

Money off many of our publications including the *Good Beer Guide* and the *Good Bottled Beer Guide*.

Access to a members-only section of our national website, **www.camra.org.uk** which gives up-to-the-minute news stories and includes a special offer section with regular features.

The opportunity to campaign to save pubs under threat of closure, for pubs to be open when people want to drink and a reduction in beer duty that will help Britain's brewing industry survive.

Log onto **www.camra.org.uk** for CAMRA membership information.

**CAMPAIGN
FOR
REAL ALE**

Do you feel passionately about your pint?
Then why not join CAMRA

Just fill in the application form (or a photocopy of it) and the Direct Debit form on the next page to receive three months' membership FREE!*

If you wish to join but do not want to pay by Direct Debit, please fill in the application form below and send a cheque, payable to CAMRA, to: CAMRA, 230 Hatfield Road, St Albans, Hertfordshire, AL1 4LW. Please note than non Direct Debit payments will incur a £2 surcharge. Figures are given below.

Please tick appropriate box

	Direct Debit	Non Direct Debit
Single membership (UK & EU)	£20 ☐	£22 ☐
Concessionary membership (under 26 or 60 and over)	£14 ☐	£16 ☐
Joint membership	£25 ☐	£27 ☐
Concessionary joint membership	£17 ☐	£19 ☐

Life membership information is available on request.

Title_____ Surname_____

Forename(s) _____

Address_____

_____ Postcode_____

Date of Birth_____ Email address_____

Signature_____

Partner's details (for Joint Membership)

Title_____ Surname_____

Forename(s)_____

Date of Birth_____ Email address_____

CAMRA will occasionally send you e-mails related to your membership. We will also allow your local branch access to your email. If you would like to opt-out of contact from your local branch please tick here ☐ (at no point will your details be released to a third party).

Find out more about CAMRA at **www.camra.org.uk** Telephone 01727 867201

* Three months free is only available the first time a member pays by DD

Instruction to your Bank or Building Society to pay by Direct Debit

 DIRECT Debit

Please fill in the form and send to: Campaign for Real Ale Ltd. 230 Hatfield Road, St. Albans, Herts. AL1 4LW

Name and full postal address of your Bank or Building Society

To The Manager Bank or Building Society

Address

Postcode

Name (s) of Account Holder (s)

Bank or Building Society account number

Branch Sort Code

Reference Number

Banks and Building Societies may not accept Direct Debit Instructions for some types of account

Originator's Identification Number

| 9 | 2 | 6 | 1 | 2 | 9 |

FOR CAMRA OFFICIAL USE ONLY
This is not part of the instruction to your Bank or Building Society

Membership Number

Name

Postcode

Instruction to your Bank or Building Society

Please pay CAMRA Direct Debits from the account detailed on this Instruction subject to the safeguards assured by the Direct Debit Guarantee. I understand that this instruction may remain with CAMRA and, if so, will be passed electronically to my Bank/Building Society

Signature(s)

Date

✂ detached and retained this section

This Guarantee should be detached and retained by the payer.

 DIRECT Debit

The Direct Debit Guarantee

- This Guarantee is offered by all Banks and Building Societies that take part in the Direct Debit Scheme. The efficiency and security of the Scheme is monitored and protected by your own Bank or Building Society.

- If the amounts to be paid or the payment dates change CAMRA will notify you 10 working days in advance of your account being debited or as otherwise agreed.

- If an error is made by CAMRA or your Bank or Building Society, you are guaranteed a full and immediate refund from your branch of the amount paid.

- You can cancel a Direct Debit at any time by writing to your Bank or Building Society. Please also send a copy of your letter to us.